So how was Occup.
It was about the [?]
in WS?

Nowhere - Everywhere

Are We the 99%?

Bridge leadership
desired, enforced as [crossed out]
documentary

Setting up safe space

Culture of

Creating statement

collective identity

Older, new [?] meet

org

HEATHER MCKEE HURWITZ

Are We the 99%?

*The Occupy Movement, Feminism,
and Intersectionality*

TEMPLE UNIVERSITY PRESS
Philadelphia • Rome • Tokyo

TEMPLE UNIVERSITY PRESS
Philadelphia, Pennsylvania 19122
tupress.temple.edu

Library of Congress Cataloging-in-Publication Data

Names: Hurwitz, Heather McKee, author.
Title: Are we the 99%? : the Occupy movement, feminism, and
   intersectionality / Heather McKee Hurwitz.
Description: Philadelphia : Temple University Press, 2021. | Includes
   bibliographical references and index. | Summary: "As the Occupy
   movements take on economic inequality, organizers must confront
   participants frustrated with inequality within the movement related to
   gender, race, sexuality, and other identities. The negotiations between
   participants over leadership, messaging, inclusivity, and harassment
   offer lessons for the future of big-tent organizing in progressive
   movements"— Provided by publisher.
Identifiers: LCCN 2020013292 (print) | LCCN 2020013293 (ebook) | ISBN
   9781439920213 (cloth) | ISBN 9781439920220 (paperback) | ISBN
   9781439920237 (pdf)
Subjects: LCSH: Occupy movement—United States. | Intersectionality
   (Sociology) | Feminism—United States. | Political activists—United
   States. | Group identity—United States. | Protest camps—United States. |
   Progressivism (United States politics)
Classification: LCC HM883 .H87 2021 (print) | LCC HM883 (ebook) |
   DDC 303.6/1—dc23
LC record available at https://lccn.loc.gov/2020013292
LC ebook record available at https://lccn.loc.gov/2020013293

♾ The paper used in this publication meets the requirements of
the American National Standard for Information Sciences—Permanence of Paper
for Printed Library Materials, ANSI Z39.48-1992

Printed in the United States of America

9 8 7 6 5 4 3 2 1

Contents

Acknowledgments

I am inspired by activists, both young and seasoned, who take up the burden and joy to change the world. Since I interviewed my initial seventy-three study participants in 2012, many movements have emerged around the world. While I have been behind my laptop, processing all the data I collected while protesting with members of the Occupy movement, many others have kept alive the vision of a more just future. Hundreds of thousands of people from New York, Oakland, Ferguson, Istanbul, Parkland, Hong Kong, and beyond have continued to discover new ways to agitate for social change. Activists from Occupy Wall Street (OWS) and a range of other social movements have stimulated my persistence and hope. Thank you for sharing with me and allowing me to write about your courageous experiences. A special thanks to Megan Wilson, who created the public art protest signs that activists displayed at encampments, in homes, and in storefronts around the San Francisco Bay Area and that appear on the cover of this book.

Joining the Occupy movement was a complex undertaking. The organizations and networks that activists created on- and offline were dense with social commentary about contemporary politics. Every Occupy movement–related event included a range of human interactions. Several mentors, teachers, and students trained me to be an ethnographer: to listen intently, question what I thought I had heard, and analyze multiple strains of a story at once so as not to take for granted perceptions about our human society. My professors and mentors Maria Charles, Melvin Oliver, Leila Rupp, and Verta Taylor helped me frame the first drafts of this book and provided resolute support for it for many years. I am especially indebted to Verta for her guidance in navigating feminist sociology and for showing me how to manage as a scholar-activist boldly and with style.

I am also grateful to my professors and colleagues at the Department of Women and Development Studies at the University of the Philippines, Diliman, where I began my graduate training. Working with Philippine women's movement participants and scholars who deployed intersectional praxis within the university and community shaped my work. Upon my graduation, they implored me to return to the United States and make change there. I hope that this book contributes to ending sexism, racism, and all forms of inequality, which has been my mission since my grassroots immersion with Philippine women's movements.

Furthermore, during my many years of schooling, especially in the fields of feminist sociology and ethnography, several professors and colleagues have been influential listeners and teachers. I am grateful for mentors, colleagues, and friends who helped me in myriad ways, including Janet Abu-Lughod, Cassie Pittman Claytor, Alison Crossley, Mary Erdmans, Corrie Grosse, Alexandra Hendley, Deborah Hobden Holbein, Kitty Kolbert, Debra Minkoff, Mignon Moore, Pamela Oliver, Elizabeth Rahilly, Jennifer Rogers-Brown, Chandra Russo, Anna Sorensen, and Ruth Wallace and more at Barnard College, Columbia University, Case Western Reserve University, the International Honors Program, and at the University of California, Santa Barbara. Thank you to my mentors and colleagues who waded through the data, analyses, and key crystalizing moments with me. You have helped me produce this intersectional and feminist analysis of the Occupy movement.

I am grateful for the editors and reviewers who helped me better convey my arguments through writing. I received key feedback and support that significantly strengthened this work during editing and review processes with Lee Ann Banaszak, Neal Caren, Holly McCammon, Jo

Reger, and Benita Roth; from Ryan Mulligan and Heather Wilcox at Temple University Press; and from the anonymous reviewers at *Gender & Society*, *Mobilization*, and Temple University Press.

Opportunities for undergraduate students to participate in original research projects are too rare. However, from the pilot study to the data collection, management of the archive of documents, analysis, and revisions, I have strived to include student researchers. They have received hands-on learning about social-science research and social movements. Research assistants continually enhanced this project. They dove into sometimes-repetitive administrative tasks to maintain its abundant data. Their curiosity and enthusiasm pushed the data analysis forward as they asked unguarded provocative questions. Thank you to Olivia Cao, Demme Durrett, Brianne Felsher, Kay Ferguson, Elena Fineberg, Claudia Gonzalez, Alyssa Hsing, Emily Jones, Kyle Jones, Emily Mahan, Steve Mateo, Zoe Nguyen, Lydia Rainwater, Erica Ramos, Jennifer Renfro, Ananya Sarker, Riley Simko, Alena Sorensen, and Zelda Vassar for your hard work.

I am obliged to those who provided research grants, which supported the data collection, management, and analysis. Thank you to Professor Dick Flacks and the Flacks Fund for the Study of Democratic Possibilities, the Department of Sociology at the University of California, Santa Barbara; the University of California, Santa Barbara, Graduate Division; and the Athena Center for Leadership at Barnard College. I am indebted to the Freedman Center for Digital Scholarship at Case Western Reserve University, including Stephanie Becker, Jennifer Green, R. Benjamin Gorham, and Anne Kumer, who expedited the creation of the digital Occupy Archive at https://doi.org/10.17605/OSF.IO/6V9ZF, a public repository for hundreds of movement documents that informed this book. In addition, I thank friends Lovella Calica, Anastasia Gomes, and Cary Shapiro, who provided room, board, and care for me in their homes while I completed my fieldwork and interviews.

Whether I was marching in the streets or puzzling through data, my family has provided unwavering love and care. Thank you to my mom and dad, Leslie and Howard Hurwitz, who have always believed in me, supported me, and valued my dreams. You have helped bring this project into being by sticking with me through all my political and personal adventures. My extended family and community, especially

Halle, Ted, Aiden, and Colton Rengers; aunts, uncles, and cousins; and long-time and newer friends have cared about me and this project. Thank you for your continued interest and support. And to Adam: you inspire me. You help me keep fighting for justice and striving to be free. I am grateful for the joy and home we give each other, which has kept me writing.

Are We the 99%?

Introduction

The Intersectional Imperative

From mid-September to November 2011, anyone walking along Broadway and Liberty Streets in the crisp autumn New York City sunshine heard chants, music, and the murmurs of small groups in passionate discussions coming from Zuccotti Park. Normally inhabited by office workers on their lunch breaks, during this period, the park was overrun with people in jeans, sweatshirts, and sleeping bags. Covering nearly every inch of the tree-dotted concrete space were folding tables, tents, and signs that declared, "This space is Occupied," and "Occupy Wall Street." A new social movement had transformed a quiet city block into a massive protest encampment.

Despite a lack of electronic sound-amplification systems, which were subject to confiscation by the police, the large amorphous group found ways to communicate and organize themselves. Men, women, and genderqueer people from a range of racial and ethnic backgrounds huddled in groups. They sang and chatted. They planned spontaneous marches and street theater performances. They debated such topics as gentrification, debt, police repression, and many others. To keep everyone fed, participants built a field kitchen and laid out vats of spaghetti, peanut butter and jelly sandwiches, and pizzas. Volunteer medics provided first aid in another tent. Two people sat behind an information table laden with flyers and pamphlets. Yogis conducted periodic meditation workshops. Other activists monitored the security of the encampments. Dozens of police officers scattered around the park's edge patrolled the gathering. Hundreds slept in the encampment, with some in the open air atop flattened cardboard boxes. Thousands of people frequented the camp. Inspired by this movement, known as "Occupy Wall Street" (OWS), people in more than a thousand towns and cities around the world created their own protest camps.

People from the communities surrounding the Occupy encampments joined in the protests, adding local flavor to each. A twenty-something African American woman wearing a red hooded sweatshirt visited the New York encampment and pinned to the front of her shirt a small patch emblazoned with "99%." Nearby, a Caucasian man with a white beard and a brown leather bomber jacket handed out flyers critiquing Chase Bank's and Bank of America's business practices. A boy of about age five ran past, caught up to a thirty-something woman walking a few tents ahead, and grabbed her hand. On concrete steps along the Broadway side of the park, nearly a hundred people gathered. Most wore jeans and t-shirts. A handful wore button-downs and khakis or pencil skirts and appeared to be on a break from the office. A few women and two genderqueer persons wore sundresses. Two people wore tattered corduroys and duct-taped sneakers. Someone wore a beret, some were in tie-dye, someone sported a Brooklyn sweatshirt, and someone else was wrapped in a thin sleeping bag. Several white men, college students, and recent college graduates lounged on the steps, yet there was little conformity to their group.

Periodically, individuals hollered, "Mic check! Mic check!" The chant signaled to others to repeat whatever was shouted next. These call-and-response "mic checks" became a voice-powered public-announcement system. Participants used mic checks to call for the start of an event or protest or to share ideas widely. A Latinx woman and an Asian woman directed small groups. Several young black men and women clustered in a couple of groups on the Liberty side of the steps. Millennial activists of many different races and ethnicities huddled together. The people spread out across the protest camp reflected the mix of ages, genders, races, ethnicities, and classes who might end up riding a subway car together. These "Occupiers" participated in workshops, meetings, and larger town hall–type gatherings called "general assemblies" throughout the day and night.

One group wore pink armbands emblazoned in black permanent marker with the words "SAFER SPACES." Responding to early reports of sexism and racism within the encampment, this group called for OWS to be an "anti-oppressive place for everyone." Led by feminists, the group organized trainings about racial justice. To prevent sexual violence, Safer Spaces members held workshops about the politics of consent. They shared their gender pronouns[1] with each other (he, she, they) to signal their acceptance of gender diversity. Some wrote and distributed a community agreement about respecting people of all identities. Other Occupy movement participants marginalized people of color or sexually harassed feminine participants; Safer Spaces responded by making an inclusive space and creating a support team for any activists who believed they needed it. As feminists who embraced the Occupy movement but recognized some anti-feminist practices among its participants, they critiqued the movement's internal dynamics like an informal watchdog. Conscious of intersectionality,[2] Safer Spaces participants were among many who argued that a movement to end economic inequality would necessarily need to eradicate gender, race, and sexual inequalities as well.

Thousands of Americans believed that this new Occupy movement held the promise of radical social change: it brought these people into the streets, moved them to sleep in tents for weeks in city centers, and allowed them to develop a new networks of friends and allies. But a movement of such diversity with ambitions to represent most Americans would need to negotiate new norms and old barriers to effectively cooperate and thrive. In what ways were activists able to break down oppressions and obstacles within the movement, and in what ways did the movement perpetuate status quo structures of inequality? What problems did they face, overcome, or fail to address as they attempted to create an inclusive multi-issue progressive movement?

The Political and Economic Context of the Occupy Protests

The Occupy movement emerged in 2011, shaped by the global financial crisis that started in 2007 and such protests as the Arab Spring uprisings from 2010 to 2011. A variety of protest tactics and organizing practices gleaned from other social movements inspired participants to develop their own innovative movement.

Beginning in late 2007, an economic slowdown termed "the Great Recession" harmed many people who would later become Occupiers. The global financial crisis from 2007 to 2011 caused plunging stock values, widespread home foreclosures, and unemployment (Reich 2011; Wilkinson and Pickett 2009). At the root of the Great Recession was the 2008 mortgage crisis. Thousands of homeowners in the United States defaulted on their mortgages, long-term housing loans issued by banks. Often, homeowners defaulted because the mortgages included hidden fluctuating interest rates, which inflated their monthly payments. Sometimes, individuals had just borrowed more than they could pay reasonably because the loans were relatively unregulated. Banks lent out a lot of money; the more they lent, the more they could profit from the interest accrued. Yet banks knew that individuals could not reasonably pay back many of these loans, especially when the adjustable interest rates on the mortgages rose. Still, with little legal regulation or government oversight of the mortgage and loan industries, banks allowed individuals to buy larger and more expensive homes or to borrow against their value with home equity loans. Due to these disreputable lending practices, property values inflated as bankers and real estate professionals realized that the banks would give larger and larger loans—until banks and individuals defaulted on these investments. The mortgage crisis caused housing values to plummet, leaving thousands of people across the United States financially insecure and disillusioned with the government for failing to regulate the banking industry.

The failure of the housing market rippled through other industries in the United States and abroad. The stock market's value fell dramatically. The mortgage crisis, compounded by gambling-style investment practices in banking and finance industries, contributed to the failure of several massive lending institutions. The Federal National Mortgage Association (known as Fannie Mae), the Federal Home Loan Mortgage Corporation (known as Freddie Mac), the investment firm Lehman Brothers, and more became insolvent; in other words, they were unable to back up their debts with cash reserves (Taibbi 2011). As stock values dropped, companies laid off workers and stopped hiring. Some companies mandated furloughs, a way to cut salaries and save on employee costs by requiring employees to take unpaid time off. The U.S. government passed the Troubled Asset Relief Program (TARP) in 2008 and the American Recovery and Reinvestment Act (ARRA) in 2009. Over much of the next decade, each stimulus package was intended to allot hundreds of billions of dollars to individuals and corporations that suffered during the recession. Yet officials designated the bulk of the bailouts to banking companies, while many individuals who lost their homes and small businesses continued to suffer.

Economies around the world struggled to recover from the Great Recession, and many governments implemented austerity measures, which cut spending on such public services as education, healthcare, and housing to redirect funds to stimulate economic infrastructure. The Greek government issued some of the first and most severe measures. Beginning in May 2010, the Greek population demonstrated in seven general strikes and many other smaller protest events, which may have included nearly one-third of the Greek population (Rüdig and Karyotis 2013a, 2013b). Soon after, in December 2010 and January 2011, frustrated by economic inequalities and their repressive authoritarian governments, Tunisians and Egyptians launched massive all-night street demonstrations. Protesters in Jordan, Morocco, Syria, and several other Arab countries joined in with parallel demonstrations throughout the spring of 2011 that became known as "the Arab Spring" or "the Arab Uprisings." After Greece, Spain became the next European country to see its population erupt in protests regarding austerity measures, foreclosures, and evictions. These citizens formed "the 15-M movement," so named because they started camping in the central plazas of Madrid, Barcelona, and other towns on May 15, 2011. They called themselves "Indignados," meaning "the outraged." International news and citizen journalists posting on Facebook and other burgeoning social media platforms publicized the worldwide wave of protests. People in many different locations around the world responded similarly to the economic downturn, austerity programs, and a desire for democracy by marching and camping in the streets overnight.

In the United States, many people studied these global uprisings and became inspired to act. Experienced feminists and civil rights movement activists discussed the demonstrations with their networks. Activists from the anti-globalization mobilizations of the 1990s and the anti-war movement of the 2000s posted messages of solidarity on Facebook. Following the global uprisings, several American activist groups organized protests in solidarity with the worldwide anti-austerity and pro-democracy actions. Activists in Wisconsin camped in the state capitol building to protest austerity measures in their state and laws that limited collective bargaining. Groups of mostly experienced activists in New York City founded the Occupy movement with the goal to be a radically inclusive response to economic and democratic insecurity—"for 99% of people."

"We are the 99%" became the key slogan of the movement. It symbolized a broad class-based solidarity in opposition to the wealthiest 1%, the government, corporations, and banks. Like the participants in the worldwide protests, Occupy activists also created encampments. Encampments became a mechanism for participants to form solidarity with others in their communities and pool resources, such as volunteers, food, and monetary donations. Participants built public awareness about the wealthiest 1% of people, who were hit by the Great Recession but able to bounce back, unlike middle-class and poor families. Occupy activists called for tighter regulations of the banking industry and fair housing practices. Participants critiqued the TARP and ARRA "bailouts." They argued that the government was assisting financial institutions ("Wall Street") more than the general population ("Main Street"). As more individuals became Occupiers, they educated each other about the Great Recession and shared the stories of their lives.

Occupiers discussed the problems of racism, sexism, and discrimination due to sexuality and disability. Many participants debated about not only the class-based troubles that had brought them together but the ways in which they could build a diverse and broad movement of literally 99% of people. They sought to end class and other inequalities in the United States and around the world. Yet as much as the movement strived to end inequalities, it was also limited by the social hierarchies that activists created among themselves. Although its members sought to create a progressive movement, the Occupy movement emerged within a society troubled by class, racial, gender, and many other inequalities. Participants often replicated the social hierarchies they claimed to abhor (Ridgeway 2011). The movement was limited by the economic and political context of 2011 and persistent social inequalities.

Despite these limitations, by camping together in public spaces, Occupiers attempted to build a small-scale "prefigurative," or ideal, society. Prefigurative politics for the Occupy movement became the ongoing daily practice of forming collectives, media, and leadership guided by egalitarian values (Breines 1989; Polletta and Hoban 2016). For many Occupy participants, an ideal prefigurative world would be based on practices copied from Argentinian and other South American social movements known as "horizontalism" (Sitrin 2012a) or forms of direct democracy (Sitrin 2012b). Participants practiced horizontalism by creating flat organizational structures. They designed team-based and rotating leadership structures instead of vertically hierarchical ones. Instead of being represented by individual leaders, horizontal organizational structures engaged a range of diverse people in decision making. Regardless of one's social position, individuals were to be respected, seen, and heard by the other participants. Attempting to flatten hierarchies and practice direct democracy, many groups developed innovative events where participants used hand signals to indicate approval or disapproval. Theoretically, anyone participating in the movement could organize a meeting or protest.

Experienced activists brought many ideas about "prefigurative politics" into the Occupy movement. Senior citizens who had participated in social movements in the 1960s and 1970s shared their knowledge from the counterculture of their youth. Anti-nuclear, environmentalist, and peace activists contributed their expertise from their prefigurative protest encampments from the 1970s to the 2010s. Anarchists and socialists contributed ideas about prefigurative politics gleaned from participating in the global justice movement since the 1990s. In addition, many recent college graduates had learned about the politics of intersectionality in classes and brought their desires for a radically new world to the movement (Crossley 2017; Milkman 2017).

The ideal world envisioned in Occupy encampments included several social and environmental innovations. Most encampments shared food and shelter among participants and the surrounding community, which encouraged many homeless persons to join the movement (Gitlin 2012; Schein 2012). In some of the larger encampments, participants peddled bicycle-powered generators to produce their own clean energy to run laptops and power social media campaigns. They silk-screened pro-Occupy images and slogans on thrift-store T-shirts. By attempting horizontal leadership and other innovations, participants in the Occupy movement tried to create a society that would serve the majority of people rather than the society that they protested, which served only the wealthiest 1%.

Yet creating a movement to serve 99% of people—let alone bring into being an ideal future world—was an extremely complicated undertaking. Groups across the country faced conflicts about how to adequately address everyone's grievances. They struggled with how to include people from many different racial and ethnic backgrounds, people of a range of gender identities (men, women, transgender persons, and people of nonconforming gender identities), and people of diverse sexualities, nationalities, abilities, and disabilities. Alongside the promise of the innovative encampments, tensions about racial and class inequality festered (Juris et al. 2012). One of the central tensions involved whether the movement truly included and represented 99% of people.

The Intersectional Imperative

Members of the Occupy movement engaged in heated debate about much more than just banking reform or building solidarity only on the basis of class identity. Infighting about class inequality and other power relations based on gender, race, and sexuality differences also influenced the movement's dynamics.

Individuals experience discrimination at the "intersection" of multiple and interconnected structures of inequality. "Structures of inequality" are practices within social institutions that perpetuate the privileging of one group over another. Using rules, laws, and cultural practices, people create and re-create groups that receive more privileges than others. Theories about who does and does not hold power and how power is systemically and unequally distributed are central to intersectional analysis. For example, redlining laws in the United States from the 1930s to the 1970s restricted the real-estate and banking industries from allowing people of color to purchase housing in more affluent and white-dominated areas, contributing to segregation (Hernandez 2009). The structure of racially and class-based inequality in home ownership continues to influence the social stratification of jobs, education, and urban development across different communities. In another example, employers, workers, and schools have designated (formally or informally) certain jobs as for women and others for men and have unequally apportioned pay and power in response. Businesses have created a structure of inequality within workplaces by holding the higher-paid, more prestigious jobs for men. Likewise, until the Civil Rights Act of 1964, newspapers printed job ads for women in a separate column from job ads for men, thereby reinforcing the gender gap in jobs along with the cultural expectation that women were only eligible for worse-paid, more menial work. Subtly and overtly, teachers have funneled boys and girls into separate career paths: boys have tended to choose male-dominated fields of study, while girls have chosen female-dominated fields that align with their gender identity (Charles and Bradley 2009). These examples illustrate just a few of the many ways in which individuals have created and re-created social structures that privilege some groups over others. To understand comprehensively how wealth and income are distributed to people in certain communities with certain identities necessitates examining not only the class structure of inequality but the privilege and oppression associated with gender and race differences.

"Intersectional analysis" means explaining privilege and oppression as a result of multiple and interrelated structures of inequality. Since the 1960s, women of color who experienced sexism and racism have focused their activism on changing multiple inequalities simultaneously. Kimberlé Crenshaw (1989) has coined the term "intersectionality" by arguing that the disadvantages that black women endure are distinct from the racism experienced by black men *and* distinct from the sexism experienced by white women. She writes that women of color experience new forms of stereotypes, discrimination, and oppression produced by combinations of racism and sexism. Crenshaw argues for an analysis of inequality grounded in people's unique experiences of multiple and interrelated structures of inequality: "Because the intersectional experience is greater than the sum of racism and sexism, any analysis that does not take intersectionality into account cannot sufficiently address the particular manner in which black women are subordinated" (140). She argues for the necessity of intersectional analyses to address the particular experiences of multiply marginalized groups, such as women of color. Intersectionality contrasts with "monist" analyses of power that only consider class inequality, only gender inequality, and so forth without considering how structures of inequality may be interrelated, compounded, or unique for people who endure multiple inequalities (Carastathis 2016; Cho, Crenshaw, and McCall 2013; D. King 1988; B. Roth 2017). At the forefront of contemporary critical feminist analysis is the idea that understanding and transforming inequality requires intersectional analysis.

Each structure of inequality privileges particular identity groups. An individual's race, class, gender, or sexual identity signals that person's connection to either the privileged or oppressed groups. In addition, identities are "multiple," meaning that individuals possess gender, race, class, sexual, and other identities simultaneously. Any one individual's experience of privileges or oppressions occurs at the "intersection" of several structures of inequality and according to one's particular identity. Typically, individuals who identify as white, heterosexual, wealthy men hold greater privileges than others, although this example can vary by context. Furthermore, within a particular context, certain scales of power or privilege may be more important than others in determining which individuals suffer more limitations (Townsend-Bell 2011). For example, in the United States, men of the racial identity dominant in a particular social movement group are likely to become the group's leaders. A black man or woman is unlikely to lead a white-dominated organization; likewise, a white man or woman is unlikely to hold a leadership position in a black person–dominated group (Morris and Staggenborg 2004). In another example, although an undocumented citizenship status may be a limitation in a social movement group that performs high-risk acts of civil disobedience due to the likelihood of arrest, undocumented youth have become the main leaders of the DREAMers movement to grant citizenship to youth born in or brought to the United States by their undocumented parents (Terriquez 2015). Therefore, one's relative privilege, such as the likelihood of holding a leadership position, depends on the structures of inequality within a particular context.

From its inception, intersectionality has been a tool for conceptualizing structures of inequality *and* changing them. While "intersectional analysis" is a cognitive and emotional evaluation of inequalities, "intersectional praxis" is the term used to indicate when individuals or groups apply what they have learned through their intersectional analysis to create strategies for social change and then act on them. Erica Townsend-Bell (2011) suggests that "intersectional praxis" includes the ways in which activists recognize and act on intersectional analyses "on the ground" in their goals, strategies, recruitment, and protest tactics. In defining "praxis," Patricia Hill Collins and Sirma Bilge argue that "intersectionality is not simply a heuristic for intellectual inquiry but is also an important analytical strategy for doing social justice work." They recognize the One Billion Rising movement against violence as intersectional: "[It] centers on the needs of women and girls, yet no one woman or category of women stands for the billion. Instead, by using the site and the day of action to draw together seemingly unrelated projects into a global imagined community, the site highlights the multiplicity of experiences that women have with violence" (2016, 58). Members of One Billion Rising coordinate worldwide dancing flash-mob demonstrations[3] against sexual violence. The campaign uses an intersectional analysis to recognize that women are not a monolith. In each protest location, organizers address women's oppressions specific to that context. Melissa Brown, Rashawn Ray, Ed Summers, and Neil Fraistat (2017) recognize that participants in #SayHerName[4] exemplify "intersectional mobilization"; the movement that recognizes the racial *and* gender dimensions of police violence and produces social media campaigns that seek justice for black female victims. The Asian Immigrant Women Advocates (AIWA) organization, based in Oakland, California, has also deployed an intersectional analysis to shape its structure, leadership, goals, strategies, and framing:

> [AIWA] does not focus solely on gender, class, race, or language, nor does it organize along single-axis identities such as Chinese or Korean or Vietnamese immigrants, Asian Americans, women, or workers. Rather, it offers participants many different points of entry and engagement at the intersections of their diverse and plural identities. In doing so, AIWA

promotes an approach to identities as tools to be used in complicated, flexible, and strategic ways. (Chun, Lipsitz, and Shin 2013, 918)

AIWA's leaders have created a culture of inclusivity with the group's goals and practices because they recognize that their members' grievances are not based on only one dimension of their identity. For AIWA members, fighting for justice and equality based on gender, class, race, language, *and* nationality has proved to be the best way to increase membership and strengthen solidarity. Using intersectional analysis that informs their praxis, they have designed an enduring organization with diverse leadership. Each case study of intersectional praxis demonstrates how activists translate intersectional analysis and theory into action for social change. Activists avoid monist analyses, they address multiple inequalities within their particular context, and they do progressive social justice work that sparks solidarity and commitment among diverse constituents.

Yet not all social movements accomplish intersectional analysis or develop their analyses into intersectional praxis. Even within so-called progressive movements, some groups do not take into account multiple structures of inequality (Carastathis 2016). For example, Amaka Okechukwu (2014) suggests that the ways in which organizations engage race, gender, and sexuality issues with their collective action influences frame resonance, who can be recruited, and who is mobilized to act. In her study of activist conferences, intersectional analysis is key to the diverse and inclusive collective action frame used by the conferences of mainly black women and men. Similarly, in their analysis of the Québécois women's movement, Marie Laperrière and Eléonore Lépinard (2016) argue that organizations use intersectionality strategically as a tool for inclusion. However, they find that not all organizations use intersectionality in the same way or to the same effect. For instance, some organizations use intersectionality to create feminist identities inclusive of indigenous women. Yet other organizations do not specifically include indigenous women and instead use intersectional analyses to argue that feminists are diverse and that feminism has no one meaning. Likewise, Benita Roth (2017) finds that Los Angeles members of ACT UP came together despite differences to form a coalition to stop the spread of AIDS and advocate for treatments, but social inequalities among the membership strained their ability to enact intersectional praxis. Furthermore, although queer black feminists spearheaded the Black Lives Matter movement and women contributed significantly to Bernie Sanders's presidential campaign in 2016, participants in both movements experienced conflicts about intersectionality, and women endured harassment and marginalization in each of the movements (Hurwitz 2019). Without intersectional analysis, activists struggle to create inclusive movement dynamics. Each of these studies suggests that intersectional praxis is uneven within progressive movements.

To evaluate intersectionality in mixed-gender mass movements requires the development of theory about the social construction of intersectional praxis within not-explicitly feminist social movements. Participants continually create and re-create collective identities, frames, cultural products and media, and even feminist activism within social movements. These aspects of social movements are products of the interactions between their participants. Participants work within each social movement's structure and the preexisting structures of inequality in their particular context. And at the same time, humans are agentic and complex. They are continually choosing how to interact with others to go along with the status quo or create new aspects of the social movement (Ferree 2009; Giddens 1990; Goffman 1959; West and Zimmerman 1987). Activists who engage in intersectional analysis examine social problems as the result of multiple intersecting structures of inequality, and they apply intersectional analysis to develop intersectional praxis, the collective actions that activists undertake to create change based on intersectional analysis.

Based on thousands of ethnographic observations collected for this study, I find that activists who utilize intersectional praxis to create more inclusive movement dynamics accomplish three processes, which I term "the intersectional imperative": (1) they address multiple forms of inequality with specificity, (2) they depict the lives and stories of people who are multiply marginalized, and (3) they encourage coalition building. Each of these processes relies on evaluating structures of inequalities as multiple and interrelated. Without the intersectional imperative, some individuals may feel excluded or become marginalized. When social movement participants embrace the intersectional imperative, activists mitigate infighting about gender, race, sexuality, and class. They strengthen the movement by creating opportunities for diverse and inclusive participation. Committed and included participants strengthen solidarity across mass movements. Whether contemporary social movements endure or fizzle depends on how their activists engage in intersectionality.

Intersectional praxis is a form of feminism that may facilitate ending sexism, racism, and all forms of discrimination, especially within not-explicitly feminist movements. Contemporary social movements are more likely to thrive when they analyze and work tirelessly to mitigate oppressions based on racial, class, gender, sexual, and other inequalities simultaneously—or, in other words, practice the intersectional imperative and feminism.

Occupy and Intersectionality

We have more to learn about how activists apply intersectionality to the everyday dynamics in mass social movements. In the Occupy movement, some participants developed collective identities, frames, and leadership that signaled the inclusion of only certain people, often using monist approaches to analyze class inequality and then mobilize. Occupiers called for mass participation but did not specifically recognize people who endured multiple forms of oppression. Often, white men, and some women, excluded men of color and women of many different races and ethnicities from leadership positions. Participants and leaders in the movement failed to address demands from experienced activists for more speaking time for marginalized persons. Many participants fell back on re-creating unequal relationships during the especially chaotic and challenging moments of protest, which threatened the movement's effectiveness and longevity (Ridgeway 2011; Swidler 1986). However, some participants *did* engage in intersectional analysis and put that analysis into practice. Some collective identities, frames, and leadership strategies aimed to be inclusive across race, gender, class, and sexual differences. For example, Safer Spaces, mentioned earlier in this chapter, evaluated gender, race, and class inequality and developed such strategies as the community agreement to bring their intersectional analysis and praxis to the larger movement. Many cisgender women, trans women, feminists, and other gender nonconforming femmes endured discrimination during the Occupy movement; nevertheless, many of them were crucial to creating and maintaining the movement and pushing for intersectionality. The meanings conveyed and symbolized in Occupiers' protests, media, culture, and collective identities often prioritized the inclusion of white men and failed to specifically include women and genderqueer persons of all races and ethnicities and men of color. Therefore, multiply marginalized activists, such as financially insecure women of color, founded alternative groups to recognize their specific identities and grievances. Participants utilized intersectional praxis unevenly across the Occupy movement, which became a source of heated debate.

Conflicts about intersectionality within the Occupy movement point to the continuing relevance of feminism and the extent of antifeminist backlash within contemporary social movements. The goals of contemporary feminism have become increasingly numerous and diverse, ranging from peace and transgender persons' rights to workplace justice and economic equality (Reger 2012, 2015). Many of these issues overlapped with the economic justice and pro-democracy goals of the Occupy movement. Furthermore, feminist principles have traveled beyond women's movement organizations and into new organizational spaces, such as mixed-gender social movements (Crossley 2017; Hurwitz 2019; Staggenborg and Taylor 2005). Yet heated debates about the relevance of feminism and uneven intersectional analysis within the Occupy movement are symptomatic of how Jo Reger (2012) characterizes contemporary feminism as "nowhere-everywhere." "Nowhere-everywhere" is the idea that feminist beliefs and actions simultaneously appear trivial and "dead" or "nowhere," yet, at the same time, they persist among women as a basis of identity, solidarity, and mobilization. While the Occupy movement was not a feminist, queer, or lesbian, gay, bisexual, transgender, and queer/questioning (LGBTQ) movement, tensions about feminism shaped the movement from its beginning.

Analyzing the Occupy movement intersectionally is important for comprehensively understanding the contemporary protest cycle. Along with the Arab Uprising that began in 2010, the Occupy movement has been the genesis of the contemporary and ongoing protest cycle. Americans moved into the streets and enlivened online networks to support the Occupy movement. Research has celebrated the movement as the first diffusion of a consensus-based "structure-lessness" participatory democracy movement in the United States in decades (Piven 2013). Occupy was the first mass movement in the United States to extensively utilize social media. A new generation of millennial activists spearheaded innovative online organizing techniques (Milkman 2017). Several of the friendship and organizational networks conceived in the Occupy encampments have continued and transformed within the contemporary protest period to influence the current political landscape. The Arab Uprising, the 15-M movement in Spain, and the Occupy movement have each been wildly popular. However, each of these movements has also been marred by reports of discrimination against women and racial minorities, suggesting that a lack of intersectional praxis has also characterized the contemporary protest cycle (Hafez 2014; López and García 2014; Salime 2012).

Progressive politics writ large depends on "big tent"[5] mass movements for its effectual and its ideological core. So as not to make the same mistakes again, we can analyze Occupy movement activists' positive and negative experiences. We must learn when some activists excluded participants and issues and weakened the movement from the inside. Occupy movement activists' experiences reveal practices that lead to exclusivity and infighting as well as insights about how to build inclusive and intersectional social movements.

The Study

As a feminist sociologist and activist, I became intrigued with Occupy activists' reconceptualization of inequality as "the 99% versus the 1%." As a graduate student in California in the late 2000s through the mid-2010s, I was concerned personally about the financial crisis and deepening inequality. As a result of the financial crisis, the University of California furloughed staff and faculty. Universities across the country began hiring freezes or limited their new faculty hires. Many turned permanent positions into contractual or temporary jobs (often relabeled as adjunct and visiting assistant professorships, lectureships, and postdoctoral positions). Like those of other Occupy participants and millennials, my future job prospects began to look uninviting. The Occupy movement reflected my personal interests in amending the growing economic inequality in the United States.

Also, the Occupy movement was extremely intellectually intriguing to me. Initially, it appeared that people of many different generations, genders, races, and class positions were coming together to participate. Simultaneously, I was discouraged to learn about reports of racism and sexism among participants. As I monitored Facebook and read activist blogs, I learned about the preeminence of white participants in movement leadership and in the encampments. I also saw reports about the lack of women participating in late-night general assemblies or overnight camping due to safety and childcare concerns. I began to see that although the movement purported to be inclusive of 99% of the population, certain groups were unwelcome or unable to participate. Some scholars and journalists argued that the Occupy movement was dominated by white men, that sexism was rampant but ignored in the encampments and movement organizations, and that feminism was peripheral to the movement (M. Butler 2011; Eschle 2016; McVeigh 2011; Montoya 2019; Pickerill and Krinsky 2012; Reger 2015). Yet others took the position that women participated in all aspects of the movement's work and that feminist organizations contributed significantly to Occupy protests (Brunner 2011; Maharawal 2011; Milkman, Luce, and Lewis 2013; Seltzer 2011; Stevens 2011). The more I heard discussions about identity, inclusion, harassment, diversity, racism, and feminism within the Occupy movement, the more interested I became in examining these debates systematically. I realized that the Occupy movement, with all its accomplishments *and* its shortcomings, was an important sociological "laboratory" in which to learn about mass contemporary social movements.

From the fall of 2011 through the beginning of 2012, I gathered and analyzed newspaper, magazine, and other web-based articles about the movement. Research assistants and I found the New York City and San Francisco Bay Area occupations to be two of the largest and most influential movements. They received the most news coverage. They modeled tactics and strategies that Occupy movements in other locations replicated. Women were involved in many of the important committees. Furthermore, in each location, participants developed organizations for feminists and people of color separate from the main movement. I developed a research plan that included traveling to New York, San Francisco, and a national Occupy conference to attend meetings and general assemblies and to find and interview active participants.

While the movement mushroomed in September and October 2011, in mid-November 2011, a coordinated effort among police and city mayors destroyed most encampments. Still, some occupations persisted through the spring of 2012 in San Francisco, Denver, Madison, and Honolulu. A scaled-down encampment remained active outside Liberty Church, a few blocks away from the original encampment in New York City's Zuccotti Park. In response to the loss of their encampment spaces in late 2011 and early 2012, many participants continued to hold citywide general assemblies and "working group meetings" (committee meetings) in alternate locations. Most shifted their tactics and strategies away from the encampment protests. They held meetings indoors for the winter. Other participants drew on the movement's online networks and face-to-face friendship groups to develop related mobilizations or entirely new organizations and protests.

According to the media and participants who engaged primarily in the physical encampments, the movement demobilized late in the fall of 2011. To those who appraised the movement as focused narrowly on class issues or the encampments, the movement did appear to contract or even die. However, discussions about the class, race, gender, and sexuality dimensions of the movement continued. Many participants remained active in organizations and protests that utilized tactics beyond the encampments. Throughout 2012 and during a follow-up study I conducted in 2016, I found activists continuing a range of Occupy-related projects and eager to reflect on how they had protested since 2011.

Having researched reports of infighting within the movement, I participated in meetings and events to observe activists firsthand. I studied the organizations and cultures of the citywide Occupy movements. In addition, I paid attention to committees run by people who identified as feminists, queer persons, and/or people of color that developed separate tactics and collective identities. I traced the movement's infighting through email discussion lists and followed up in person with participants to learn more about the conflicts. I sat down with seventy-three activists in 2012 to discuss their participation in depth. Because many of the interviews revealed a variety of conflicts within the movement, interviewees selected pseudonyms that I have used throughout the book to ensure confidentiality.

The research questions that guided my study initially[6] primarily addressed infighting about gender discrimination. Yet the many feminists with whom I spoke viewed their work and the problems within the movement intersectionally. As my study progressed, I broadened my original list of research questions and examined the Occupy movement intersectionally to address larger concerns: How do Occupy movement participants build solidarity across gender, race, class, and sexual identities within the mass movement? Under what conditions do movement cultures exclude or alienate particular individuals and groups? How do gender, race, class, and sexuality processes influence contemporary social movements' dynamics and culture?

To research these questions, I used a critical feminist approach to social science, which meant continually checking and balancing my standpoint as a participant and researcher and conducting research to contribute to social change (Blee and Taylor 2002; Taylor 1998; Taylor and Rupp 2005). When I attended events or meetings, I disclosed that I was a participant *and* a researcher.

Unlike most movement participants, I continually, reflexively, and critically studied the movement from my perspective as a researcher. By being a researcher in the movement, I became an "outsider," unlike other activists participating as concerned citizens whose main objective was making social change (Taylor and Rupp 2005). During every event and protest, I jotted notes about the proceedings, went home afterward, wrote up my notes, and questioned what I had observed. I was also an "outsider" because I was constantly conducting interviews. These research activities helped me reflect about the movement, the participants, and myself. Using this outsider's perspective, I conducted my research with what scholar Donna Haraway (1988) calls "passionate detachment," a subjective, embodied, and critical research process.

Although I was an outsider researcher, I gained an insider perspective because I was an active participant in meetings and protests.

With my goal to write a book about the movement, my role as a participant *and* a researcher was similar to that of participants who wrote articles, blogged, created reports, and developed other media for and about the movement. My socioeconomic class status and education level also made me an insider among the large percentage of participants who were graduate students and professionals (Milkman, Luce, and Lewis 2013). Like many Occupiers, I felt empowered to join an important moment in history.

Similar to participants in this study, I helped organize among the grassroots, locally and nationally. When I was not in the field in New York or San Francisco, I was a student and instructor at the University of California, Santa Barbara. I participated in Occupy Santa Barbara meetings and protests. I shared information about nationally important protests, such as the Strike Debt campaign and the Occupy National Gathering (NatGat). Likewise, when I attended events and meetings in my field sites, I reported about Occupy Santa Barbara activities to provide a perspective on how the movement persisted in smaller cities.

In a movement with many men and not many explicitly feminist participants, I felt peripheral, or a modification of the idea that Patricia Hill Collins (1986) calls "outsiders-within," participants in organizations who are not completely comfortable or accepted.[7] I was apprehensive about where to sleep when I visited encampments. I was irritated when I was interrupted during meetings by more aggressive male activists. When I visited protests, I received unwanted sexual advances. Similar to the participants in this study, I felt a mix of joy, fear, pride, and frustration by participating in and researching the Occupy movement. Likewise, when I immersed myself in the interviews and field notes that described other participants' experiences of racism, sexism, and harassment, I felt emotionally drained, depressed, angry and sad. These feelings sparked my sociological imagination.[8] While conducting this study, I drew on my experiences as a feminist, participant, researcher, and "outsider-within" to keep a critical distance from my research. I analyzed my personal reflections and the larger social structures of the social movement. I paid attention to the inequalities in which the movement was situated. In addition, I compared on-the-ground observations collected at three of the national Occupy movement's key field sites.

The Field Sites: Occupy Wall Street, Occupy Oakland, and the Occupy National Gathering

I conducted research for this study at OWS in New York City and the San Francisco Bay Area, especially Occupy Oakland (OO), as well as at NatGat in Philadelphia. New York City and the San Francisco Bay Area were home to the largest, most prominent, and most diverse city-based Occupy encampments in the United States (Gitlin 2012; Graeber 2011; Mahler 2012; Milkman, Luce, and Lewis 2013; Pickerill and Krinsky 2012; Van Stekelenburg 2012). Both sites were the subject of national media attention due to their participants being the most politically savvy and the most heavily policed (see, for example, Gillham, Edwards, and Noakes 2013; M. King 2013). The occupation locations became what Aldon Morris (1986) has termed local "movement centers," or the most influential activist locations that catalyze and sustain a larger movement. The Occupy movement in New York City and the San Francisco Bay Area deployed notable tactics and strategies in each location that ignited the nationwide movement.

The Occupy movement benefited from resources, leaders, social movement communities, and creative populations in New York City and the San Francisco Bay Area. Each city is a vital center for social movements. Populist activism and the civil rights, lesbian and gay rights, women's rights, and labor movements developed in and continue to thrive in each city. Additionally, both cities are home to large creative populations known for setting trends in media and fashion (Cohen 2008). These creative populations helped make the movement more attractive to mainstream audiences. They facilitated the diffusion of protest through social media (Pickerill and Krinsky 2012; Van Stekelenburg 2012).

Although the cities are dissimilar in some of their leading industries, both serve as hubs for the finance and banking industries that were targeted by Occupy. The San Francisco economy is concentrated around the technology industry, while New York City has long been a leader in textiles, fashion, advertising, entertainment, and publishing. However, each city has established global financial districts and large commercial ports for international trade. On each coast of the United States, Occupy participants created movement centers that targeted significant financial and banking districts and ports (Wollan 2011).

The field site at NatGat in Philadelphia included an assembly of participants from the nationwide movement. In the first summer of the movement in 2012, participants from the New York City and San Francisco Bay Area movements joined key informants from smaller cities, such as Denver, Atlanta, Houston, Cleveland, and Philadelphia. Organizers from smaller and midsize cities traveled to NatGat to exchange information and strategies with other Occupiers and participate in mass demonstrations and national action plans. NatGat also gave Occupiers who had mainly participated in the movement on Facebook, Twitter, and InterOccupy, the social media hubs for the movement, the opportunity to meet in person. NatGat occurred at a crucial moment in the life of the Occupy movement: nearly one year after the movement's emergence and at the beginning of the decline of the outward mass mobilization. NatGat provided a face-to-face meeting for activists who had been working together nationwide but mostly online. A large portion of the four-day conference's schedule was devoted to a "visioning" process, or a way to reframe the movement's goals. Activists aimed to create a resurgence of activity or at least solidify the movement's organization and goals so that the Occupy movement could persist nationwide in a cohesive manner.

Occupy Wall Street

The New York City encampment, OWS, has been the focus of scholarly research and journalism. OWS started the movement and was established at the location of the main target of the movement: the U.S. financial, investment, and banking epicenter on Wall Street. The protest encampment was located in Zuccotti Park, three city blocks from Wall Street and the New York Stock Exchange. Protesters marched in and around the financial district daily.

Throughout September and October, thousands of adherents visited the OWS encampment. Bystanders stopped by the encampments to observe the movement's festivities. Many joined discussion circles, watched artistic performances, and even protested. Scholars estimate that several hundreds and possibly as many as two thousand activists gathered in the first forty-eight hours in mid-September to create the New York encampment (Gitlin 2012; Milkman, Luce, and Lewis 2013). On October 1, 2011, fifteen hundred protesters marched through the financial district and onto the Brooklyn Bridge, where police arrested seven hundred marchers (Baker, Moyinihan, and Nir 2011; National Public Radio Staff and Wires 2011). The protest gained international media attention and led to more than six hundred solidarity protests around the United States and globally by October 9, 2011 (J. Butler 2012). Dozens of working groups and committees created a vibrant community at OWS, offering daily musical performances and organizing general-assembly "town-hall" meetings.

Although protesters cleaned and monitored the camp rigorously, on November 15, 2011, New York City officials ordered police to dismantle the encampment, citing unsanitary health conditions, unsafe structures, and potential fire hazards (Liboiron 2012; Lubin 2012). Police used force and tear gas to clear the park of protesters and then hauled away $100,000 worth of tents, sleeping bags, other equipment, and more than two thousand books from the OWS library (Reuters 2013). Protesters were never able to permanently reoccupy the encampment after the mid-November dispersal because police barricaded the park with orange mesh construction fencing. However, since November 2011, protesters have held several one-day protests in Zuccotti Park. Additionally, they have held one-day encampment reunions, called Occupy Town Squares, in parks across New York's five boroughs. Other Occupy activists remained politically engaged and active through 2016 in Occupy spin-off projects (sometimes no longer classified as part of the Occupy movement but nevertheless originating in it) and in activism related to Bernie Sanders's 2016 presidential campaign.

Occupy Oakland and Occupy in the San Francisco Bay Area

San Francisco Bay Area Occupy movement supporters created encampments in downtown San Francisco on September 17, in Berkeley on October 8, and in Oakland on October 10, 2011. Each encampment was a short subway ride from the others. Although participants typically joined one of the three encampments, they also traveled between the encampments to participate in events, protests, and meetings. Each of these separate but connected protest camps benefited from long-standing radical political communities and progressive social movements local to the area.

Since the 1960s and 1970s, the San Francisco Bay Area has been renowned as a seedbed for social movement communities, including the radical student community at the University of California, Berkeley (UC Berkeley); the Free Speech movement; and notable protests of the Vietnam War. A center for the civil rights movement, Oakland is also the location of the historic headquarters of the Black Panther Party and the Ella Baker Center for Human Rights.

In the contemporary period, anti-police brutality and student movements galvanized San Francisco Bay Area activists. Participants in anti-police brutality and anti-racism movements held heated protests in response to the mistaken fatal shooting of Oscar Grant III by the Bay Area Rapid Transit police in 2009 (Bulwa and Swan 2018). The protests took place in and around Frank Ogawa Plaza, a city green space and amphitheater across from Oakland's city hall, which activists dubbed "Oscar Grant Plaza" to memorialize him. Participants in the Oscar Grant protests established the plaza as a well-known public square for progressive communities. Occupy Oakland would grow by establishing the Oakland encampment, later called the "Oakland Commune," in the same plaza and initiating rallies and marches from the plaza's amphitheater. Many participants in the anti-police brutality movement would become participants in Occupy Oakland.

Students also fueled the emergence and development of Occupy in the Bay Area. From 2009 to 2012, UC Berkeley students protested tuition hikes and budget cuts threatening the California education system. The movement politicized a new generation, which organized students across the state of California. Many of its participants and student leaders would contribute to the emergence and growth of the Occupy movement in San Francisco, Oakland, and Berkeley (Kingkade 2011). Progressive and racially diverse communities in the San Francisco Bay Area, especially in Oakland, contributed to a base of support for the Occupy movement (Mahler 2012).

Occupy protests in the San Francisco Bay Area fueled the movement's strength and popularity, encouraged movementwide solidarity, and generated compassion for protesters in opposition to forceful policing. Like the Zuccotti Park encampment, the San Francisco encampment was one of the first occupation sites but would become one of the longest running. The encampment persisted in two different locations in the city's financial district. Activists would switch locations when police would power-wash one encampment space in the middle of the night, demolish tents, and threaten protesters with arrest.

San Francisco Bay Area activists, especially those in and around Oakland, contributed heavily to cultivating the Occupy protest culture. Although the national movement was initiated by activists in New York City, Oakland activists created enormous excitement about it (Mahler 2012). At the Occupy Oakland encampment on October 25, 2011, police fired tear gas, bean bags, and other projectiles to disperse protesters. One of these projectiles struck Scott Olsen, an Iraq War veteran; he was hospitalized for more than a week as doctors induced a coma to heal the resulting brain injury (T. Collins 2011). This incident inspired many area Iraq War veterans, among others, to deepen their solidarity with the Occupy movement to oppose the violent policing. On November 2, 2011, Occupiers demonstrated their power and popularity by blockading the Port of Oakland, the fifth-largest seaport in the United States (Wollan 2011). Activists who participated in the blockade—or "General Strike," as activists termed it—marched through the streets and climbed atop shipping containers. These high-risk tactics generated great compassion and solidarity among other Occupy activists across the United States and around the world.

The National Gathering

From June 30 to July 4, 2012, NatGat occupied two different parks in Philadelphia. The first day, participants met on the grassy "mall" adjacent to the museum that houses the Declaration of Independence and coordinates an annual government-sponsored celebration of Independence Day. The government runs the park, which is open to the public, but NatGat organizers did not secure a permit to erect tents, set up camp, and hold their demonstrations. During the first day of the gathering, park police and other social movement groups persuaded NatGat to relocate to make way for other groups that had obtained permits for protest spaces. For the remainder of NatGat, participants shifted a few blocks away to a privately owned park that did not require a permit for protesting. The NatGat encampment provided free meals, free camping space in the Quaker Friends Center's overflow parking lot, and cultural performances for attendees and passersby.

By bringing together key informants from across the nation, Nat-Gat aimed to focus Occupy's goals as a national movement. From approximately 10:00 A.M. to midnight each day, NatGat organizers arranged dozens of speakers, working group meetings, and workshops. Roughly ten small group meetings occurred every hour throughout the encampment. Via conversations, teach-ins, presentations, cultural performances, and working group meetings, participants shared movement tactics, strategies, and goals. The meetings and events trained local leaders in Occupy's politics and procedures. For example, they held workshops on how to "move your money" from corporate banks that abetted the mortgage crisis into local credit unions. And they practiced effectively using hand signals during general assemblies to aid the consensus decision-making process (Cagle 2011). Each evening, participants held general assemblies. Afterward, choirs, theater troops, and comedians entertained the encampment. Organizers scheduled mass rallies and marches each evening, but throughout the day, working groups, committees, or groups of friends spontaneously marched en masse through the streets of Philadelphia. They rallied in front of a Wells Fargo bank branch, a Fox News affiliate station, and branches of other multinational corporations and financial institutions. Symbolically, NatGat "Occupied the Fourth of July" by creating a series of pro-democracy protests that disrupted and critiqued the government and corporations before and during Independence Day festivities. Similar to the Philadelphia gathering in 2012, activists convened in the summer of 2013 in Kalamazoo, Michigan, and in the summer of 2014 in Sacramento, California, to protest and conference for the Occupy movement.

Organization of the Book

Occupy participants in each field site socially constructed collective identities, media and culture, leadership, and feminist actions. Some participants developed innovative intersectional praxis within the mass movement. Other participants did not approach activism intersectionally and even perpetuated social inequalities. Chapter 1 provides an intersectional analysis of the movement's collective identities. In an attempt to move beyond racial, gender, or sexual divisions, Occupy participants developed the 99% identity. However, for many participants, labeling the movement identity as "the 99%" obscured diversity within the movement. Participants argued that lumping everyone under "the 99%" failed to specifically recognize women's of various racial and ethnic backgrounds and other people of color's distinct experiences during the financial crisis. The chapter explores how groups emerged from within the movement and developed oppositional collective identities. They formed solidarity based on their specific shared class, gender, race, and sexual identities in critique of the "We are the 99%" umbrella and the Occupy movement's identity.

Chapter 2 describes the range of media, frames, and cultural products that Occupy participants developed. Participants' media generally conveyed one of three messages about inclusion and diversity. First, participants developed cultural products to broadly celebrate the 99% identity. However, this 99% frame did not specifically identify class, gender, racial, and sexual subgroups or avenues for coalition building. Second, media resonated with the androcentric and male-dominated cultures of finance and banking to target these strongholds of the wealthiest 1%. However, media that used the dominance frame ostracized participants who were not white, male, or wealthy. Third, women and genderqueer participants of a variety of racial and ethnic identities especially recognized the subordination of their ideas, bodies, rituals, and emotions in the first two types of cultural products. In response, these participants created media and cultures that specifically represented identities and inequalities intersectionally by using an intersectional frame. These media creations not only supported the Occupy movement but also sparked coalition building with the feminist, transgender rights, racial justice, and lesbian and gay movements.

In addition to a movement's collective identities, media, and culture, the ways in which leaders and followers interact reflect whether a social movement uses intersectional praxis. Chapter 3 explores the movement's intertwined leadership and followership through an intersectional lens. The Occupy movement subscribed to "leaderlessness" or a "horizontal leadership structure," wherein anyone was welcome to volunteer for leadership positions. Without a set leadership hierarchy, participants aimed to involve people of multiple diverse backgrounds in leading the movement. To understand who led and how they did so, this chapter examines followers' interactions with leaders, which were informed by cultural beliefs and inequalities about gender, race, and other identities. When individuals acted on prejudices, they created "discriminatory resistance," a term I coined to indicate when followers impede leadership in particular from women and genderqueer persons. In any particular context or group, gender, race, class, age, or a combination of identities may form the basis for cultural standards of leadership. In the Occupy movement, many followers opposed women and genderqueer persons' leadership attempts and rewarded men's leadership practices according to traditional gendered and raced hierarchies. Even within a movement that claimed to be horizontally organized, participants marginalized women and genderqueer leaders, especially people of color, rather than facilitating diverse leadership.

Chapter 4 exposes how many of the conflicts around the intersectional imperative explored in previous chapters sparked feminist activism. The chapter reveals the feminist resources and organizations outside the Occupy movement that contributed to its development. Separate feminist mobilizations emerged from within the movement and reinvigorated unrelated feminist organizations and networks. Three processes were central to feminist mobilization and the adoption of the intersectional imperative in Occupy: (1) the construction of feminist collective identity, (2) the creation of feminist free spaces,[9] and (3) the actions of feminist bridge leaders. In fact, the sexism, racism, marginalization of queer people, and harassment that existed within Occupy provided a political opportunity for activists to take a stand for intersectional feminism.

Finally, the Conclusion provides lessons gleaned from conflicts within the Occupy movement, which can help future social movements avoid infighting and deploy the intersectional imperative. Future social movements that strive for diversity and inclusivity must embrace the intersectional imperative when they create collective identities, media and culture, and a leadership structure. Occupy was one of the largest outpourings of populist activism in the United States in decades and helped usher in the contemporary protest cycle. Remnants of the Occupy movement fueled activism after 2012, most notably support for Bernie Sanders's 2016 and 2020 presidential campaigns, which continued to oppose the "1%." However, the unexamined scars of the Occupy movement have led to the replication of its mistakes throughout the contemporary protest wave. I compare my findings about intersectionality—or the lack thereof—in the Occupy movement to its presence in other contemporary protest movements nationally and globally. The intersectional solidarity *and* conflicts observed through this study are common in the Indignados movement in Spain, activism related to the uprisings popularly known as the Arab Spring in the Middle East, #BlackLivesMatter, and the Women's March that started in 2017. The methodological appendix that follows provides a detailed description of the study's data, methods, and analysis.

1

Are We the 99%?

Conflict about Collective Identities

Evelyn, a middle-aged white woman from the San Francisco Bay Area, was already active in several nongovernmental organizations (NGOs) when she joined the emerging Occupy movement. She contributed food, spread the word about the movement among her online network of friends, and brought other activists to the protests. Even though she did not sleep over at the encampments, she explains the variety of ways in which she felt that she was really a part of "the 99%":

> I attended the GAs [general assemblies]; I cooked and took food once or twice a week; I had individual conversations; [and] I was involved in helping to create a coalition called the San Francisco 99% Coalition, which is people from the Unitarian church, labor organizations, and various other organizations that are in support of the Occupy movement but are not doing encampments. That was kind of a bridge between this new movement—literally living on the streets—and the more traditional NGO interests and other kinds of organizations.

Evelyn not only contributed to the collective identity of the 99% but also helped develop partner organizations, such as the 99% Coalition.

She recognized that some activists in her network from labor movements, churches, and nonprofit organizations would not feel comfortable sleeping in the encampments but should be included in the Occupy movement. Later, as reports of harassment and the underrepresentation of women in the movement surfaced, Evelyn shifted her organizing focus toward Women Occupy, a group created to increase women's involvement in the Occupy movement despite complaints about sexism in the encampments. She built connections between feminists within and outside the movement. While Evelyn saw herself as a part of the 99% collective identity, she contributed to the development of groups that included older participants and women, for whom sleeping overnight in the urban encampments was more difficult.

Evelyn's reasons for shifting her work away from the main movement's organizations and toward alternative groups contrast with the reasons that Lola contributed to Occupy and racial-justice organizations. A participant in Occupy Oakland (OO), Lola summarizes her own personal experience with racism:

Lola: Different groups of people left for different reasons. I think that they just were not willing to acknowledge, understand, and dialogue about issues of racism within the movement.
Interviewer: Did you personally experience someone not addressing race issues well?
Lola: Yeah, I feel like I experienced that a lot [laughs abruptly]. Yeah, and a lot of the time, it was more like people would disregard what I said or what I felt or my thoughts. It wasn't that they were being outright racist—it was that they didn't take me seriously. I'm a small black woman, and I'm not super outspoken, but when I feel like I have a very strong conviction, I feel like I have to make myself heard. So sometimes, people would disregard me, because I came across as like some "angry black woman" stereotype. . . . I think everyone there at some point was guilty of failing to understand others. Or groups of people failed to understand how to address their own ignorance about other people. Even a few times I would completely disregard someone, because I would say, "That's a white man, so what he says doesn't matter to me, because there's no way he could understand me."

Lola's experience is representative of the racial tensions within the movement. Lola considered herself an Occupier and contributed to social media activism. She collaborated almost exclusively with activists who were people of color. And yet Lola debated constantly whether to stop being an activist. Lola fought against being silenced by white activists, men, and anyone else who stereotyped and ignored her as just another "angry black woman." She found that splinter groups from the main movement that focused on racial justice better represented her identity and grievances. Members of organizations dominated by people of color were more likely to respect what she had to say. Furthermore, they were developing connections with other racial-justice organizations, which Lola believed was necessary to expand the Occupy movement.

While Lola and Evelyn expressed solidarity with Occupiers, they also critiqued and opposed the movement. By developing separate women's, feminist, and racial-justice groups, they each rejected the 99% identity as being too narrow to encompass their own grievances, identities, networks, and preferred strategies of activism. Due to their social locations as women with particular racial and age identities, Lola and Evelyn were not satisfied with the generic Occupy identity and contributed to the development of intersectional collective identities. While Women Occupy examined the intersection of gender and class inequality, the People of Color Caucus (POC) focused simultaneously on racial and class injustices. These women's experiences represent two of the ways in which Occupy participants utilized intersectional analysis, rejected the 99% identity for organizing only on the basis of class, and practiced that intersectional analysis in the form of developing oppositional collective identities.

Oppositional Collective Identities

Within a social movement, the process of defining "us" versus "them" is the process of forming a collective identity. Studies of many social movements have revealed that the process of becoming a group is wrought with internal conflicts over who is included, how to set the boundaries, and how and whether to act as a cohesive group (J. Gamson 1997; Ghaziani 2008; Hunt and Benford 2004; Melucci 1985; Rupp and Taylor 1999; Taylor 1996; Taylor and Whittier 1992).

Oppositional collective identities are critiques of the main move-ment's collective identity. Participants in lesbian, gay, bisexual, trans-gender, and queer/questioning (LGBTQ) and feminist movements have long debated how to manage multiple and opposing collective identities. Often, participants have disagreed about who should be included in or excluded from these movements and created oppo-sitional groups to air their grievances and find space for their own identities (Ghaziani 2008; Montoya 2019). Although some collective identities emerge from participants who have engaged in intersec-tional analysis and translated intersectionality into practice, other collective identities involve only select groups.

Participants in social movements socially construct their collective identities. They develop consciousness about their shared grievances, create a boundary around who is included and who are their targets, and perform that collective identity by protesting, wearing certain clothes, or completing other actions that identify them as belonging to the group (Taylor and Whittier 1992). For example, participants in the January 2017 Women's March on Washington formed a collec-tive identity as a women's movement in opposition to President Don-ald Trump's administration, and many wore "Pussyhats" to visually demonstrate their solidarity as part of the group. The hats' wearers wanted to reclaim the idea of vaginas or "pussies" as being powerful in response to misogynist statements made by Trump about grabbing women "by the pussy." Women around the country, and some men, furiously knitted these hats in anticipation of the march. Bird's-eye photos from the march show thousands of people wearing bright pink caps, performing their collective identity. However, some feminists viewed these Pussyhats as a form of exclusion. Some argued that the march was too white, even though it was led by several women of color (Rose-Redwood and Rose-Redwood 2017). They argued that the Pussyhat symbolized white women's vaginas and performed the march's collective identity of solidarity for white women at the ex-clusion of people of color, indigenous women, men, and transgender persons. They argued that many vaginas are not pink. Women have vaginas of many colors. Men and transgender persons may or may not have vaginas but may want to join the movement. The Women's March was a mass social movement, with women and men of a vari-ety of races and ethnicities participating, and those wanting a more

intersectional message of inclusivity opposed the Pussyhat's representation of the march's collective identity (Boothroyd et al. 2017). From
nearly the first call to action, the media and activists used an intersectional lens to debate about the movement.

Although debates about collective identity are not new (Reger
2012; B. Roth 2004; Upton and Bell 2017), conflicts about forming
solidarity across gender, race, class, and sexual differences remain
salient in contemporary activism. Amin Ghaziani (2008) suggests
that conflicts about including people of many different identities
in LGBTQ marches on Washington produce liveliness and debate
that strengthen the movement. However, in the Occupy movement,
conflicts that sparked oppositional collective identities tore at the
broad solidarity implicit in the 99% identity. Unlike movements that
serve a group of participants who share some life experiences, such
as LGBTQ movements for sexual minorities, mass movements aim
to bring people of many different identities together who may share
few if any life experiences.

Occupy activists attempted to create a radically inclusive collective identity with the idea of the 99%. This concept symbolized a mass
movement open to everyone except the wealthiest 1% of people. However, for many participants, the Occupy movement obscured diversity by not specifically recognizing groups of people with particular
experiences. Activists like Evelyn and Lola, featured at the beginning
of this chapter, advocated for collective identities based on intersectional analysis, because the broad mass movement's identity did not
represent their particular grievances and life stories or readily involve their networks. Several activists recognized the 99% collective
identity as a monist analysis rather than an analysis that recognized
gender and race as important axes of inequality. For these activists,
class was not the only analytically important category, and activism
needed to reflect multiple categories of difference (Townsend-Bell
2011; Montoya 2019). Using the internet, Occupy activists were able
to air and spread their grievances unlike members of any previous
movement. Recirculating critiques on Facebook and blogs, participants in the movement entered a constant state of critique. As activists formed oppositional collective identities, the intersectional
imperative they advocated reached the oppositional groups but not
the main movement's organizations. Participants created a range of

different subgroups that more specifically addressed the racial, gendered, and sexual dimensions of class inequality. Although conflict within social movements is normal and expected, the oppositional collective identities that developed within Occupy led to fissures, separate movements, and the evasion of intersectional praxis within the main movement.

This chapter's five case studies of collective identity formation within the movement address multiple questions: How did Occupy movement participants build solidarity across gender, race, class, and sexual identities within the mass movement? Under what conditions do a movement's cultures exclude or alienate particular individuals and groups? First, Occupy activists explain their support for the 99% identity that characterized the main movement's organizations. In the next four cases, activists who intersectionally analyzed class inequality describe how they modified the 99% collective identity and to address the racial, gendered, and sexual dimensions of class inequality. These four cases present groups that developed what F. Tormos (2017, 712) describes as intersectional solidarity: "recognizing and representing intersectionally marginalized social groups formed by multiple interactions and linkages between different social structures and lived experiences." People with submerged race, gender, class, or sexual identities within the movement sparked oppositional collective identities to represent their specific experiences of inequality, stemming from more than just economic imbalances. These oppositional groups sought to include people by specifically recognizing class, race, gender, and sexual inequalities as multiple and interconnected. Yet when participants formed oppositional collective identities, they typically left the main movement's organizations. This process led to the weakening of the central Occupy movement and the flourishing of new grassroots organizations with collective identities that worked to fulfill the intersectional imperative.

"We. Are. The 99%!"

By participating in the everyday life of the movement and protesting together, participants developed identities as part of the 99%. Estrella, a Chicana[1] woman from the western United States, explains becoming awakened to activism:

For a lot of people, this was their first go in public organizing. I remember at first, there were these discussions where people would say, "Can we do this?" And people would say to them, "Of course you can. Let's find people. Let's do it. Why couldn't you?" It's like people—and I include myself in that group of people—who have a hard time feeling free. What does that mean to say I have some power? Even what would it look like if we made something happen?

For Estrella and many others with whom I spoke, the range of issues that the movement addressed were foundational to the 99% collective identity. They educated each other about why they should protest. They recognized their ability to act collectively on their grievances. Estrella and others listened to and learned from each other to better identify with the 99%. Jayne, a white woman from the western United States, is representative of several people with whom I spoke in emotionally describing her decision to join the movement:

Always, no matter which Occupy, or what Occupy event that we go to, it feels like home in a way, because you know your thoughts are safe. The way that you feel about the world is safe. You know that it's just open. Everyone thinks something different, so it doesn't matter. That was nice for me, just coming around to having a safe place.

Jayne's consciousness about being a part of the 99% centered on the movement's inclusivity and intention to create change. She recognized Occupy protests and meetings as spaces where anyone from the 99% could share ideas and be heard. Estrella and Jayne suggest that participants realized the significance of forming a new movement and became politically and emotionally connected to each other.

Participants formed the 99% collective identity as a boundary to separate the richest 1% from everyone else. Catherine, a Latina woman from New York, explains why many participants adopted this identity in opposition to the 1%: "I feel connected to the 99%, because most of us are poor. And we are the ones being oppressed. And then there's the 1%, [who] just care about themselves." Catherine was conscious of economic hardship and believed that the idea of the 99% versus the 1% represented an important boundary between people who were struggling financially and those who controlled the majority of wealth in the United States and globally. Likewise, Alan, an Asian man from Oakland, elaborates a commonly held sentiment that the 99% identity created consciousness about the movement's targets and how to create social change: "When I started seeing the 'We are the 99%' rhetoric coming out of New York, I thought, these people really get it. So many institutions are built on a foundation of money. We need to challenge the underlying power relationships, and that's why I wanted to be involved." Alan believed that the 99% identity created consciousness among Occupiers to protest the long-standing power held by financial institutions, banks, and large corporations. The movement's framing and discourse resonated with participants, like Catherine and Alan, who saw themselves as a part of the 99% collective identity.

Singing, marching, and doing other activities en masse became moments for participants to develop solidarity that transcended individual differences. Sandra, a long-time activist with the Raging Grannies social-justice and protest performance group in New York City, explains how collective identity developed among Occupy participants in the protests:

> I got them singing—I said come on, come on, you can sing along. It was we [the Raging Grannies] who wrote "Solidarity Forever." I started waving my arms—I was a grandma—and it was like their mother telling them to do something, so finally, they did it. And by the end of it, there were so many hundreds of kids sitting out in the middle of the late fall, and they were singing along—there was this enormous sound—and when we got to the end of it, there was this big roar.

In Sandra's view, hundreds of participants in the encampment created unity across gender, race, class, disability, organizational, and generational differences by singing and protesting together. Likewise, Rachel, a white Jewish woman from San Francisco, describes the moment when she felt connected with OO:

I think, of course, the most inspiring thing was the port shutdown. I mean, that was amazing to see so many people in the streets, people that you know—all my friends were in the streets, and people that would never go to protests were involved. You know, people just came out. It was a really massive populous moment, and I was very excited to be a part of that.

For many protesters, the Port of Oakland, a major shipping hub for global trade, symbolized the 1%. Historic protests like shutting the port down allowed the 99% to act collectively against the 1%.

In addition, participants organized online to amplify their support for street protests. Danielle, a white woman from the western United States, explains how she adopted the 99% identity by participating in social media with a large number of other Occupy supporters. Inspired by the success of the New York City encampment, she describes trying to participate in the movement with others online:

> I pulled up the livestream and was obsessed for three days. In the first days, $2,800 of pizza was delivered to Zuccotti Park. I was thinking—people are supporting this! This is really going to happen! We have a shot! So I started hashtagging all over the place—I was just learning Twitter; I got onto Twitter because of Occupy Wall Street. I started hashtagging #Occupy on everything in my state that I could think of—the tourist center, the airport, all of these organizations. I was just like [makes sounds as if typing furiously]. Within a few days, I was getting people responding. So I was like, let's meet Saturday, September 24. And we did. And that's how it happened.

Danielle publicized the movement using the #Occupy hashtag. She exchanged information with people online, grew conscious about the movement, and felt a sense of belonging with the 99%. Then she met the people she Tweeted with, and they started an encampment in her town square.

In the streets and online, participants grew to identify with the 99%. Dramatic gatherings like the encampments and the port shutdown were opportunities for people build solidarity as part of the 99%. By educating each other about economic inequality and organizing online and in the streets, participants constantly created and re-created the meaning of the slogan, "We are the 99%." However, not all participants felt included in the newly formed collective identity. When some participants viewed the 99% identity as narrowly defining class and lacking intersectional analysis of the inequalities that structured their lives, they began to develop oppositional collective identities.

The Racial Dynamics of the 99%

Decolonize Oakland

OO became an epicenter of debate about how a mass movement could include people of many diverse gender, racial, class, and sexual identities. From the movement's inception, activists debated whether it was inclusive of people of color. Participants in Oakland, a racially diverse city undergoing aggressive gentrification, led the national Occupy movement in debates about racial inclusivity.

One of the most poignant examples of contentious infighting about how to create an inclusive prefigurative society focused on the presence of indigenous people. Participants debated whether and how the movement addressed their specific economic and democratic grievances and how to form coalitions with experienced indigenous activists (Barker 2012; Campbell 2011). Illustrative of this debate was a poster created by Jesus Barraza and Melanie Cervantes, both members of the artist collaborative Dignidad Rebelde. The poster features a man in a feather headdress and embellished vest typical of the Ohlone Native Americans indigenous to the San Francisco Bay region. The image is silk-screened over a drawing of downtown Oakland's skyscrapers. Across the top of the poster runs the slogan: "Oakland is Occupied Ohlone Land. Decolonize the 99%. Defend Mother Earth." Activists displayed prints of the poster at encampments and spread the image through social media.

The images in the poster encapsulate an internal movement debate: whether Occupiers should change the name of the entire movement from "Occupy" to "Decolonize." Activists of color argued that framing the movement as an occupation undermined hundreds of years of work by indigenous people in opposition to "occupation," another word for the wrongful colonization of their land by the U.S. government. These debates critiqued the 99% collective identity as excluding people of color's specific experience with racial and class oppressions. Molly, a mixed-race part-indigenous activist who watched this debate closely and participated in it online, explains, "There was huge conflict with the concept of the word 'occupy' and how we are on occupied [Native American] lands already. Right from the beginning, we said, 'This is not the best name, and these are the connotations that go with this word 'occupy.'" Molly explains a widely held sentiment among many indigenous people and people of color in the movement: that "occupy" was suggestive of the violent colonial history of the United States. Labeling the mass movement as "Occupy" contradicted the creation of an inclusive organization. A blog post by Morning Star Gali on an OO website recapitulates the debate:

> While we know that "Occupy" is the terminology used around the country to explain and unify this movement, it does not address the real issues of colonization that happened in this country and particularly to Oakland and the Chochenyo Ohlone residents of this city. . . . Changing the name to "De-Colonize" is an innovation that would also speak to the brilliance and community of OO to address the current issues of gentrification in Oakland and the social problems that gentrification have perpetuated as well as pay homage to our revolutionary ancestors who fought for a better, more inclusive and respectful Oakland.[2]

Morning Star Gali argues that the Occupy movement's organizers ignored an intersectional analysis of racial inequality and genocide in the United States. Like many people, she opposes the undertones of white supremacy embedded in the framing of the movement. Moreover, she compares the nationwide problems of the Occupy movement's name to local problems of racialized inequality in Oakland. She argues that the Occupy name is comparable to the gentrification in the San Francisco Bay Area that transformed communities like the once Latinx-dominated Mission District into a community of white, millennial, technology-industry workers with skyrocketing rents.

During interviews and in the field, participants often discussed how to create a movement that would include people of diverse racial backgrounds and build coalitions with other racial-justice organizations. Lively face-to-face discussions at general assemblies addressed the Occupy name, how activists were organizing and outreaching, and the media's portrayals of the movement. For example, the OO December 4, 2011, general assembly began with drumming and Native American chants. Individuals stood up to explain what the Occupy movement meant to them. Everyone listening repeated their words using the "mic-check" tactic:

> Mic check—hello, my name is Luca, [and] I'm Ohlone [indigenous]. . . . [W]e thought that it was important that those who are newly oppressed should help and listen to those who have the wisdom and have been oppressed for over five hundred years.

Others spoke, allowing the crowd to listen to several sides of the debate:

> Mic check—my name is Emiliano. I respect the goals of introducing decolonization in a more visible way to this movement. . . . I think occupations when they are military occupations, as we see in places throughout the world, are objectionable. But the use of "occupation" in the original attempt of Occupy Wall Street was for people to occupy the seat of power. So I don't think we should get too caught up on the word. And I would recommend that the debate be framed not as either occupy *or* decolonization but [as] occupy *and* decolonization.

Murmurings, side conversations, and debate within the crowd continued. More people stood up and spoke:

> Mic check—my name is Wilson. Wall Street is about a wall that was built to keep the indigenous people out of the U.S. area. The first stocks were interests in slave ships that were traded on Wall Street. What we are about, in our opposition to Wall Street, is about that system. . . . Albuquerque has already

changed their name to "Unoccupy." Other Occupies are also using different names. Here in Oakland, we have to be sensitive to decolonization, which is about decolonizing our minds. Words are important if we are going to decolonize our minds.

Participants at the assembly called for a reenvisioning of their prefigurative world with much greater attention to racial inequality and the history of colonialism. The debate about whether to create a more inclusive name, such as "Decolonize" or "Unoccupy," or to keep the name "Occupy" to be in solidarity with the worldwide movement was one of many conflicts about racism. As Adam Barker (2012, 331) summarizes in his in-depth analysis of the Decolonize movement: "For Indigenous peoples, these discourses must seem at turns ironic and absurd: privileged Settler people play-acting at freedom while Indigenous peoples' own . . . governance ha[s] been derided and attacked for centuries." Due to the variety of ways in which participants excluded racial minorities, many activists, especially people of color, left the main Occupy groups and formed the Decolonize oppositional collective identity.

The Decolonize Oakland group evolved from the People of Color Caucus (POC) and the Queer People of Color Caucus (QPOC) in OO. Decolonize Oakland aligned with a variety of people of color's and immigrants' organizations in the city and provided a place where women-of-color feminists could organize to simultaneously draw attention to racial and class inequalities. The group supported such activities as an immigrants' rights march on May Day 2012, a coalition against a rate-swap deal between the city of Oakland and Goldman Sachs that cost Oakland residents millions of dollars, and internal movement gatherings, such as a group discussion of Gloria Anzaldúa's (1987) classic text, *Borderlands/La Frontera: The New Mestiza*. Members of Decolonize Oakland often participated in other groups that also developed oppositional collective identities, such as Occupy the Hood[3] and Roots, each of which drew heavily on preexisting mobilizing structures in African American communities in Oakland, such as civil rights organizations and the network of black churches.

Led by several women and queer participants, Decolonize Oakland rejected the primacy of the class-based 99% collective identity. Jesse explains the boundary between participants in Decolonize, who acted on their political consciousness about intersectionality, and other Occupy activists, who focused narrowly on class inequality:

> Some of the white Occupy guys think this is the moment where we have to deal with the cops and anti-capitalism. And we've been told things like—I can't even believe that people have said things like—"You guys have to wait until after we deal with this, and then we can deal with race and gender." And I'm like, "Are you serious?!" That's what people thought in the '60s, that's so old school, like women-of-color feminism never happened.

Jesse's experience suggests that some of the "white Occupy guys" ignored the intersectional analysis of women-of-color feminism. The majority of participants in Decolonize Oakland drew on anti-racist, intersectional, and feminist analyses. They developed protests for economic justice that recognized the racial and gendered dimensions of class inequality. Furthermore, they recognized the lives and stories of multiply marginalized participants in opposition to mainstream Occupy "guys," who focused primarily on class and anti-capitalism. Decolonize participants sought specifically to recruit women of color and consider their experiences and grievances.

Opposing Racism from within Occupy

In several U.S. cities, people of color, including indigenous people and anti-racism activists of many different racial backgrounds, developed groups that opposed racism and white privilege from within Occupy. Roots, POC, QPOC, Occupy the Hood, and Decolonize groups prioritized the intersection of racial and economic justice. For example, the OO Foreclosure Defense Group focused on justice for people of color who faced evictions and foreclosures. They used vigils and legal tactics to stop Zaki Alshalyan, an Iraqi immigrant, and Jodie Randolph, a woman of color, breast-cancer survivor, and small-business owner, from being evicted from their homes. Activists who were conscious about racialized economic disparity created collective identities to represent their multiple grievances. As Amity puts it on the POC Working Group forum, they were "a group dedicated to educate, organize, & to mobilize the revolution. Taking it directly into the black household. By any means." Whereas the 99% collective identity did not explicitly include people of color, such groups as the POC Working Group advocated explicitly for the inclusion of people of color in the Occupy movement.

Racial-justice activists developed oppositional identities due to their conviction that building collective identity only on the basis of class without examining participants' distinct ethnic and racial experiences perpetuates racism. Vilma elaborates the tension between supporting and critiquing Occupy based on race consciousness:

> Occupy made these overt attempts at creating spaces of inclusion in a way that might seem to be politically correct. I haven't experienced racism in Occupy, I don't think, but we Latinos have a more complicated read about our place in the movement. There are so many gray areas. There is a difference in tone or rhetoric from second- or third-generation Latinos in the U.S. who have been brought up in a certain activist culture; older Latinos who have been living here for generations who really identify more with the politics of their countries of origin and their kind of, like, baby boomer activist culture that was really going on before Occupy. Then you have a lot of younger people, who are usually students. There are a lot of different ways people understand themselves as political subjects. But there are people outside of it who are just like, "Oh, great, Spanish speakers are here, we are more diverse than we thought." In this context, in some sense, empowerment feels condescending—but I guess it's healthier than, you know, retrograde racist perspectives.

Vilma explains feeling hypervisible and like a novelty within the Occupy movement. She laments that participants saw the presence of "Spanish speakers" as surprising, indicating that this group was unexpected rather than a necessary part of the 99%. Vilma captures a widely held sentiment: that the distinct experiences of Latinos from various ethnicities and immigrant generations were not specifically incorporated into the Occupy movement, suggesting that the 99% identity did not represent Latino activists comprehensively. Scholar

Eduardo Bonilla-Silva (2006) classifies experiences of racial exclusion, such as Vilma's experiences, as "colorblind racism" (see also Beeman 2015). When activists ignore the persistence of racial inequality or assume that people of color can equally participate in a social movement, they practice a passive but insidious form of racism that perpetuates white culture as expected, accepted, and ideal when compared to people of color's cultures.

Across the country, groups developed oppositional collective identities centered on racial justice to oppose the "colorblind racism" that emerged within many of the main Occupy groups. For example, the (un)Occupy Albuquerque group distributed a pamphlet titled, "FAQ (un)OccupyABQ" to expose myths about colorblind racism:

> Q: We're all humans—I don't see color. Can't we just come together as one?
> A: Sure, as long as we do so without erasing the histories and current lived realities of oppression that exist among us. . . . If we just say we are "all the same," we ignore or minimize the differences between us and refuse to accept very real power imbalances; this means it will be difficult to come together to effect change. . . . [W]e need a braver, deeper view of the world.

This pamphlet brought race issues to the forefront of activism in Albuquerque in the fall of 2011. The members of (un)Occupy Albuquerque made conversations about the intersection of racial and class inequality central to their collective identity.

In contrast to the 99% identity emerging from a culture of white privilege in which the politics and priorities of white participants were held as central and those of others as marginal, some groups explicitly embraced people of color's identities. These groups supported the economic-justice mission of Occupy but only with the unequivocal inclusion of people of color. Occupy the Hood's mission statement is representative:

> It is imperative that the voice of POC [people of color] is heard at this moment! . . . We are our future and we possess the energy needed to push the occupy movement to the next phase.

> We are The Least Represented. . . . We are Considered The Mi-
> nority. . . . But most importantly WE ARE THE HOOD!!

Instead of stating, "We are the 99%," Occupy the Hood created the "We are the hood!" collective identity, making black culture central to their organizing. Occupy the Hood participants prioritized people of color's grievances about economic injustice. They contributed to and transformed the Occupy movement by advocating for an end to racism as being essential to the end of class inequality. Kayla, a mixed-race woman from New York, explains:

> If there is racism happening within the movement, then the People of Color [POC] Caucus should call it out. We did outreach to people of color, black people, Latinos, Asians, anyone who was coming into Occupy. It was very segregated. So we had a POC labor subgroup and a POC students' group. It was a little more safe for people of color. There was less racial tension. Sometimes people needed a space where there are just more people of color around, and they would then push out into the larger groups. The first POC Working Group, maybe twenty people showed up. The people that were at that first meeting have become very close friends of mine. Then we had two hundred people at the second meeting trying to figure out what we were going to do with all of these people of color at Occupy. We got into a big old circle, and the group decided to be closed only to people of color—only people who identified as persons of color could participate and be present at the meetings. Anybody else would be asked to leave, which was difficult, because there were a lot of issues that were very contentious. Occupy was supposed to be for 99% of people, but there were people of color in Occupy who didn't completely have a say.

Although the media and scholars have largely overlooked people of color's distinct experiences within Occupy, Kayla explains the critical racial-justice and inclusion initiatives that people from a range of racial and ethnic backgrounds undertook within the movement. People of color groups collective identities symbolized an opposition to the white-dominated 99% identity. Yet although people of color created oppositional collective identities to advocate for racial equality within and outside Occupy, infighting about racism within the larger movement tended to marginalize their contributions.

Opposing Police Brutality and White Privilege

One shared experience among people of color that facilitated the development of solidarity was their experiences with police harassment and brutality. People of color were more likely to endure punishments when they performed high-risk protests as compared to white male activists. Due to this inequality during street protests, some people of color rejected the 99% identity that was based on participating in high-risk, all-night protest camps. Lola explains the conflict between people of color organizers in Oakland and white Occupy participants:

> There was this march planned for May Day that they do every year from East Oakland to downtown, and most of the organizers were Latino. They wanted to get a permit for Oscar Grant Plaza [where the Occupy Oakland/Oakland Commune encampment had been]. The general assembly at Occupy Oakland wanted to participate in the march but was insulted that the May Day march organizers wanted a permit. The Occupy activists were kind of like, "Fuck the police, we don't ask for permits, we don't ask for permission." But the people who were organizing the march wanted a permit, because a lot of the people who were going to be in the march were immigrants who were here illegally. I felt it was really insulting to the longtime organizers, telling them what they should and shouldn't do and making these arguments. I was just like, "You should defer to their judgment."

Lola argues that white protesters could participate easily in protests without the threat of deportation or jail time. However, black, Latinx, and undocumented persons were more likely to endure police brutality and arrest. Conscious of racial inequalities even within progressive protests, Decolonize and Occupy the Hood participants strategized permitted marches rather than high-risk confrontations with the police. They argued that it was important to create an environment to protest safely and lessen the possibility for arrest. They built solidarity among undocumented persons, veterans of the civil rights movement, black and brown communities, and members of black churches.

The proliferation of oppositional collective identities according to intersectional analyses of race and class created profound tension within the Occupy movement. While Decolonize members provided constructive critiques about racial tensions within the main Occupy movement, they believed that the movement did not adequately address their critiques. As a result, many people of color limited their involvement with the Occupy movement and developed alternative organizations. The creation of oppositional racial-justice organizations and the lack of anti-racist response from participants in the Occupy movement's organizations illustrate Emahunn Campbell's (2011, 50) argument that the Occupy movement's developing and weakening was devastatingly shaped by white privilege:

> These individuals, whose very social reality as white people, allows them closer access to institutions of capital and the power that is closely associated with these institutions, cannot afford and will be unable to continue this movement without a full acknowledgement, critique, and dismantlement of white privilege within its ranks. As it currently exists, the Occupy movement is hypocritical in its anti-racist stance.

Infighting and segregation within the Occupy movement greatly contributed to its demobilization. The main movement's organizers lost momentum because they could not—or would not—relinquish their "colorblind" white control over Occupy's collective identity, framing, and leadership. Furthermore, when proponents of the 99% and Occupy identities did not develop an intersectional analysis, the main movement's organizations lost the activist participation of people of color, who shifted their energies into separate racial-justice groups. Although police heavily patrolled the Occupy encampments in October and November 2011, city mayors evicted several of the largest urban encampments in November 2011, and winter weather impeded activists, racism also weakened the movement from the inside. A little more than a year after Decolonize was created and the Occupy movement had faded from the media, Black Lives Matter emerged. Many former Occupy participants welcomed this new movement that prioritized the experiences of people of color.

The 51% of the 99%

In addition to analyses about race, activists advocated for gendered analyses of class differences. Instead of the gender-neutral 99% identity, Women Occupy advocated for the 51% collective identity to make visible women's participation in the movement and their specific gendered, economic, and political needs. Activists in Women Occupy promoted the 51% collective identity to signal that women are 51% of the population and should have been 51% of the Occupy movement. For example, two women at the International Women's Day march in San Francisco on March 8, 2012, held a sign proclaiming, "51% of the population, 17% of Congress" to call attention to women's being half of the population but sorely underrepresented in leadership positions in workplaces and politics. This 51% identity highlighted the disconnect between the 99% and women's issues. It created an oppositional collective identity centered on women's unity within the Occupy movement.

Feminist bloggers expressed the need for separate groups to address women's particular identities and grievances beyond the gender-neutral idea of the 99%. The 51% collective identity signaled that women should have power equal to men's within the Occupy movement. In an article titled "Why I Broke Up with the Bank of America," CODEPINK[4] and Occupy activist Rae Abileah (2012) writes:

> Women Occupy is asking people to cancel their big bank accounts on March 8th and move their money to local banks or credit unions. Not that another reason is needed to move your money, but why not do it on a big day of action [International Women's Day] and in solidarity with the 51% of the 99%.

Abileah appeals to women as a group to support Occupy on International Women's Day by joining "move your money protests," a grassroots tactic to defund banks that took advantage of customers during the 2008–2009 financial crisis. By closing accounts with Chase, Bank

of America, Wells Fargo, and other large banks and instead supporting local credit unions, activists sought to take power away from the
big banks, one savings account at a time. In her blog, Abileah also
draws on the emotion cultures of heartbreak and girl power to advocate for Occupy participants' righteously "breaking up" with the
big banks as they would end relationships with reprehensible boy-
friends. Similarly, *Ms.* magazine's website ran a series of blog posts
on gendered class inequalities, sexism within the Occupy movement,
and feminist protests in support of Occupy. By creating the 51% collective identity, participants recognized the intersection of class and
gender inequalities, which encouraged members of other feminist
and women's groups to join the Occupy movement. Feminist blogs
became a space for consciousness raising about women's oppositional
collective identities.

Participants who had worked in feminist movements particularly critiqued the 99% identity as being too broad, too vague, and
therefore exclusive. They argued that the movement marginalized
women's particular economic experiences and ignored gender inequality. Joan, a middle-aged white Jewish woman from New York,
explains how she became involved in women's and feminist groups
within Occupy:

> I [had] never considered myself a feminist until I came to
> Occupy. I was one of those folks who thought that we didn't
> need feminism anymore. Then I noticed in Occupy that there
> were a lot of off-handed remarks and behaviors and down-
> right crimes against women. We as a group started to really see
> feminism as the great equalizer, as opposed to being all about
> women. There is a lot of talk about the gender binary. Femi-
> nism is about being more inclusive. It's more about addressing
> the dominant paradigm, because ultimately that is what causes
> inequalities. Men suffer from patriarchy as well.

Joan and other female activists formed groups focused on women's
and feminist issues to amplify women's participation in the Occupy
movement. Using gendered classed analyses, they mobilized around
how the financial crisis affected women.

Women- and feminist-dominated groups challenged the idea that men were the ideal Occupy activists. Kay, a white woman from a city in the eastern United States, recognized a lack of women's voices, ideas, and participation in Occupy. Drawing on the political consciousness she developed as an experienced activist in feminist and lesbian movements, she explains the benefits of separate women's groups:

> When women get together in groups of themselves, they empower each other. They have more strength than when there are men around, who can plunge in there and take over. Like in women's colleges, in all women's groups, women's voices are going to be heard. It should be an environment that would promote women's chances to explore things. To say things. To get ideas and then have that affect the work that they do out in the larger movement.

Due to her consciousness about the marginalization of women in mixed-gender groups, Kay advocates women's separate groups. Also, Lauren, a white middle-aged bisexual woman from New York, recognizes the solidarity she felt with the other organizers of the heavily women-dominated Feminist General Assembly group: "We really had really good feelings there. We were working together. There was a real sisterhood thing. It was palpable, this sisterhood." Many Occupy participants argued that the movement's leadership and culture was male-dominated, except in the feminist and queer committees and in some groups that focused on racial justice. Laura, a Latina woman from San Francisco, encapsulates the idea that the inclusivity of the 99% actually masked the problem of male dominance in the movement:

> How are women, women of color in particular, or people in the LGBT community being included? I think there was an assumption that it was like, "Everyone's on board!" But it's like, "Well, no, not everyone is on board." The 99% is a diverse group of people, and the problem keeps coming up that the movement is led by white males.

Like many participants in Occupy, Laura expresses concerns that the majority of leaders and speakers were men. Groups for feminists, queer persons, and people of color allowed a space for marginalized participants to develop solidarity.

Exemplary of oppositional collective identity formation was the development of the Women Occupying Wall Street (WOWS) group. Infighting strengthened the bonds between members of WOWS: although cisgender and trans men critiqued the group because it excluded them, WOWS members held to their collective written constitution that specifically included cisgender and trans women. WOWS members also fought for their group's inclusion on the Occupy Wall Street Spokes Council, a collection of affinity groups that took responsibility for maintaining the Occupy movement after the destruction of the encampment at Zuccotti Park. In the process of developing the Spokes Council, heated debates ensued as to whether groups that formed unity around particular identities should be allowed to participate. Initially, the Spokes Council included the main movement's committees, such as facilitation and media groups that did not explicitly organize intersectionally. WOWS members staged a walkout of the Spokes Council meeting when they were initially denied the right to participate because of their focus on addressing cisgender and trans women's experiences of economic inequality. WOWS members' walkout and group constitution created a boundary between them and participants in the main Occupy movement, especially men. Yet the walkout made a powerful statement and led to WOWS's eventual inclusion in the Spokes Council.

By putting forward analysis of women's economic position at the intersection of gender and class inequalities, groups developed collective identities that would appeal specifically to women and feminists. Women created their own oppositional collective identities where they could be leaders and prioritize gendered economic grievances. Several participants critiqued the 99% identity as focused on class to the exclusion of women's issues. Furthermore, they critiqued the 1% as not only elite but typically white and male. Women's and feminists' protests exposed the lack of gender consciousness within the broader Occupy movement yet used its momentum and feminist organizing to form coalitions with feminist movements. As participants in such groups as WOWS strengthened their "sisterhood," they shifted their energies away from the main movement's organizations. Similar to the Decolonize collective identity, the 51% of the 99% revealed the limits of the 99% identity and its lack of intersectional analysis or praxis.

Queering Occupy

Like anti-racism and feminist activism, LGBTQ activism was submerged within Occupy. White heteronormative masculinity dominated the movement, while queer sexualities and identities were marginalized. In contemporary U.S. society, many people held prejudices against lesbian, gay, and queer persons. The open and porous nature of the Occupy movement, which encouraged 99% of people to join, implicitly invited homophobic anti-LGBTQ participants *and* LGBTQ persons. Without assurance that the Occupy movement specifically accepted LGBTQ persons, several queer participants feared hostilities, harassment, and violence from members of the main movement's organizations and encampments.

The LGBTQ persons who joined the Occupy movement created protests from within the movement that advocated for change at the intersection of sexual and class inequalities. They revealed the economic hardships endured among marginalized LGBTQ persons. For example, they protested the lack of health care for human immunodeficiency virus/acquired immunodeficiency syndrome (HIV/AIDS) survivors and the disproportionate violence and poverty afflicting transgender persons. In addition, LGBTQ persons who were Occupy participants critiqued aspects of gay culture that they viewed as elitist, such as the expectation that participants in gay pride festivals and parades should attend expensive parties afterward. From 2011 to 2012, the media focused intensively on LGBTQ activism for the legalization of same-sex marriage in the United States (Bernstein and Taylor 2013). Yet most LGBTQ Occupy activists received less media attention because they focused on goals unrelated to same-sex marriage such as critiquing economic inequality among LGBTQ persons.

The 99% collective identity did not signal explicit support for queer participants. Infighting emerged within some encampments about whether the Occupy movement accepted and advocated for LGBTQ rights. Kasie, an Asian American woman from the San Francisco Bay Area, elaborates:

There was this issue with putting a rainbow flag on the website. Some guy was screaming bloody murder that we should not put that rainbow flag on there, because that's not what the Occupy movement represented. But this was Occupy San Francisco, the city with the largest homosexual population in the U.S., so putting a rainbow on the site was just considered normal.

As Kasie recounts, even in the San Francisco Occupy encampment—set up in the city with the largest gay population in the United States—support for gay rights was not an initial and defining feature. Yet in cities with large LGBTQ communities, such as San Francisco and New York, activists demanded that the Occupy movement support LGBTQ rights and movements. Similarly, Frank, a person who chose only to be identified by a pseudonym and not any gender, race, class or sexual identity, attended the Occupy National Gathering (NatGat) and explains the tension around LGBTQ organizing within the movement:

> Personally, I think there could have been more focus on queer subjectivity or queer issues. I know at the National Gathering, there was an LGBTQ caucus and at least one workshop related to LGBTQ issues. They talked a lot about their coming-out stories. Also, at the Feminist General Assembly at Nat-Gat, they spoke to gender issues and queer issues, which was something that I was really happy about. It wasn't just about a cultural feminist perspective, but they were looking outside of the paradigm of the man and the woman. But, in general, anything that's related to queer issues tended not to be associated with Occupy, because most of those organizations were not particularly related to a queer audience.

Lesbian, gay, and transgender participants created oppositional collective identities, such as the LGBTQ caucus, within Occupy to represent their particular experiences of inequality and involvement. As Frank emphasizes, the Occupy movement's broad goals of achieving economic justice for the 99% did not resonate with LGBTQ participants' particular grievances. Exercising the intersectional imperative, these activists created events to specifically include lesbian, gay, and transgender persons in the movement. Due to these tensions, they shifted their resources away from the main Occupy movement's organizations and toward groups that specifically included queer communities and concerns about economic justice for them.

LGBTQ participants developed email discussion lists, social media, LGBTQ and feminist groups, and events dedicated to queer leadership and politics. The Queer/LGBTIQA2Z[5] Caucus, QPOC Working Group, and a variety of feminist organizations created their own oppositional collective identities to represent queer sexualities. The Queer/LGBTIQA2Z Caucus met consistently in the fall of 2011. As reported in its meeting minutes from November 27, 2011, the group celebrated an individual's coming out and gender transition with "Jenn's Unveiling Party"; discussed how to participate in World AIDS Day on December 1; and endorsed the International Day to End Violence Against Sex Workers on December 17. To improve safety for LGBTQ participants in Occupy, caucus members published a list of "Queer Friendly Sleeping and Showering Spaces." Individuals and groups from the wider LGBTQ community also contributed to Occupy. For example, Justin Vivian Bond, dressed in drag, led a sing-along celebrating "high-heeled trannies"[6] and a new economy without the 1% as part of Occupy Wall Street's (OWS's) recognition of the National Transgender Day of Remembrance, on November 13, 2011. Representatives from the Sylvia Rivera Law Project, an organization that provides legal assistance especially to transgender, intersex, and gender-nonconforming individuals, joined OWS to conduct a "gender self-determination" teach-in on October 26, 2011. One of the leaders of the teach-in, Regina Gossett, wrote an open letter in the first issue of the *Post Post Script* zine to advocate for the inclusion of transgender and queer participants and leaders and not replicate the mistakes of the LGBTQ movement, which initially marginalized Sylvia Rivera.[7] When participants created LGBTQ-themed protests, they contributed to Occupy and LGBTQ activism and prioritized queer and transgender leaders. Many of these groups recruited participants from LGBTQ organizations to join Occupy, built solidarity among queer communities and allies, and addressed sexual and gender discrimination within the larger movement and beyond. Groups with LGBTQ oppositional collective identities became prefigurative spaces for innovative connections between Occupy, queer, and transgender activists that participants felt were otherwise suppressed within the broader 99% movement.

The signature tactic whereby participants exercised their Queering Occupy collective identity and brought together the Occupy and LGBTQ movements were Occupride protests. In a http://www.portlandoccupier.org blog post dated June 16, 2012, Sarah Morrigan, an Occupy participant in Portland, explains their purpose:

> The strongly commercialized overtone of the Pride parade and festival is taking the real spirit of the Pride—camaraderie, solidarity, community, and, yes, pride—away from the events. No one should feel like they should "pay to be gay"—that they cannot be a member of Portland's queer community unless they have money to spend on anything from booze to a gay cruise ship package. . . . By occupying the Pride, we do not mean "protest the Pride," but rather "reclaim the Pride and make it ours." Money out of Pride—it should not be an advertising campaign for any business that can afford to buy a booth or a float. This year, I call on the queer communities of Portland to truly celebrate our strengths and pride. For up-to-date Occupy The Pride Portland information, please visit http://occupridepdx.wordpress.com. In addition, some members of Sisters In Strength, Women of Occupy Portland, are planning to join the Dyke March Portland on Saturday, June 16.

Gay-pride parades are yearly festivals and marches in cities across the country to celebrate gay identity. Occupy activists who formed Occupride contingents within gay-pride parades protested the commercialization of these demonstrations. Occupy activists joined LGBTQ activists to address financial issues affecting communities of sexual minorities. Gay-pride marches in the summer of 2012 became a mobilizing structure for the continuation of Occupy protests. Occupiers critiqued the 1% within the gay community and the participation of Bank of America, Chase, Citibank, and other big banks and corporations in gay-pride events. Their slogans included "Pro-Fabulous, Anti-Capitalist," "Tax Wall St. End AIDS," and "Queer Occupy Wall Street targets a Gay 1%." The Occupride identity created a boundary around Occupy participants who sought to form coalitions with

LGBTQ organizations as they voiced the particular economic hardships endured by sexual minorities.

Exemplary of intersectional praxis sparked by the partnership between LGBTQ activism and the Occupy movement is a statement of coalitional support published on the DC Trans Coalition blog on October 7, 2011, titled "Trans People Say: End Economic Inequality, Solidarity with the 99%!" This statement declares the DC Trans Coalition's solidarity with the Occupy movement and elaborates each movement's influence on each other:

> As a whole, socially-marginalized communities (such as low-income trans people and trans people of color) suffer the most directly from poverty and are the most likely to be impacted by inequalities that arise from economic injustice. The DC Trans Coalition's major priorities—as decided upon by our grassroots base through community forums and consultations—are creating inclusive, accessible jobs and services for all marginalized people in the District. We thus stand in solidarity with the grassroots Occupy Together movements.

In this statement of solidarity, the DC Trans Coalition specifically mentions trans persons' particular identities and inequalities, intersectionally links transgender issues with economic issues, and calls for coalition building "in solidarity with the grassroots Occupy Together movements." The DC Trans Coalition is an instance of LGBTQ activists partnering with Occupy protesters to address sexual and gender minorities' particular economic and political grievances within the context of the mass multi-issue mobilizations.

The 99% Is Not One Class

Distinct Class Inequalities

Conflicts about how to understand contemporary class inequalities sparked disagreements and oppositional collective identities even from within the Occupy movement, which centered on an inclusive class identity. Across many different Occupy locations, interviewees reported tensions between homeless populations and housed participants. Some encampments displaced long-established camps of homeless persons. On the other hand, some housed activists formed partnerships with and supported homeless participants. Nancy, a white woman from the western United States, discusses the many tensions about class differences:

> Don't confuse the type of occupation that we had in the later days with the earlier days. The early tent occupation was different—it was, like, very housed. The later days were very homeless. To varying degrees, throughout the entire time, homeless folks participated in the general assemblies, which has always been a source of tension. But they were there sleeping for Occupy. I talked to most of the ones that slept there who were either part of the "twenty-four-seven committee" or many homeless women who were happier and safer because there was a community at Occupy. It was not the dark corners, alleyways, and down by the river—that was just way less safe.

Nancy credits the homeless population with maintaining the visible and high-risk protest encampment in her city as well as providing a safe space for female homeless persons. Also, she identifies a difference between the fall protests and those in the winter. In the fall, participants from a range of class identities left their houses and pitched their tents in the town square. But in the later stages during the harsh winter, the encampments became dominated by homeless participants. Despite the cold, homeless persons found purpose and safety at Occupy encampments. In the winter, Occupiers who could do so, slept and held committee meetings inside. Homeless participants contributed to the Occupy movement in the form of "sleepful" protests, or holding down encampments all through the night. Their identities as homeless and their practice of protesting all day and night, seven days a week, led to the formation of their oppositional collective identity: "twenty-four-seven Occupiers."

Homeless participants were extremely visible, and yet they rarely took on leadership positions within the main movement's organizations. Although Occupy did provide some social services to homeless persons, these were generally temporary and did not comprehensively address housing problems plaguing American cities (Schein

2012). Homeless participants responded by forming coalitions with homeless social-movement groups from outside the Occupy movement, such as churches with a mission to serve homeless persons and the Picture the Homeless group in New York City. By forming oppositional collective identities, such as twenty-four-seven Occupiers, participants highlighted their specific class identities, grievances, and contributions to the Occupy movement. Even within the 99% movement, homeless persons tended to be marginalized by housed participants.

Participants entered the Occupy movement with varying levels of consciousness about poverty. For example, Paz, a white female student from New York, argues that the 99% identity obscured the class distinctions she felt within the movement:

> He came from this really wealthy background, and I came from this extremely poor background. But he was addressing poverty and class issues in this way where I was like, "Do you hear what you're saying? You have no idea what it is like to grow up in poverty and how hard I worked."

Paz explains that creating unity across diverse class backgrounds was difficult, because many participants lacked consciousness about poverty, homelessness, and joblessness. She argues that the 99% identity painted too inclusive a picture, because it did not capture the depth and specificity of economic inequality, including her own life experiences. As a result of her disagreements with the broad 99% framing, Paz turned to the concurrently mobilizing Montreal student movement for inspiration. In the spring of 2012, Canadian students performed raucous "casserole" marches, so named because they re-purposed and clanged pots and pans, to demand universal free education. Paz spearheaded solidarity marches and actions at Occupy encampments to specifically address poverty among students, an issue that she believed was not given enough attention by the broader 99% movement.

Similarly to students, musicians formed their own demonstrations to advocate for economic concerns linked to music education. For example, after NatGat, approximately seventy-five people began the 99 Mile March from Philadelphia to New York City. The march was spearheaded by Guitarmy, a subgroup within OWS that built solidarity among musicians for the movement and serenaded encampments and marches with protest music. Participants marched in solidarity with NatGat and to celebrate famed folk-rock musician Woody Guthrie's hundredth birthday. A press release on http://occupywallst.org explains the march's goals:

> Along the way we hope to raise awareness of the importance of music as part of our civic culture, and discuss the negative impact of the erosion of public arts education funding in the last decades. Each mile that we march we ask to have sponsored by supporters through a walk-a-thon for the K–12 school instrument donation group Mr. Holland's Opus Foundation.

The marchers called for support of musicians' particular economic needs. Although they contributed to the momentum of Occupy and NatGat, participants in Guitarmy and the 99 Mile March developed separate oppositional collective identities to represent their particular class interests as musicians.

Activists developed oppositional collective identities by bringing together people with particular economic experiences, including musicians, homeless persons, and students. These groups made visible specific class identities. They raised detailed concerns about pressing economic issues among people of different class positions that were otherwise subsumed in the "economic-justice" language of the overall movement. In addition, they formed coalitions with groups from outside the movement. When individuals' personal experiences and consciousness about class differed from the main movement's broad analysis, participants often created a boundary between themselves and the 99%.

Class Analysis beyond Just the Great Recession

Especially in Washington, DC, and New York, participants created anti-war protests within Occupy encampments to advance a class consciousness based on more than just foreclosure, the mortgage crisis, and the 99% identity. For example, Prema, a queer South Asian woman, supported and participated in the Occupy movement, yet she found knowledge about class inequality lacking within it. She argued that the root of class inequalities in the United States and globally was the U.S. military industrial complex, not only the 2008 financial crisis. She explains:

> Occupy talked about austerity measures and foreclosures, which were important. But they were connected to war. But in Occupy, there was some resistance to talking about the war, unlike during the George W. Bush administration, where mass protest was anti-war protest. The banks and the government profit immensely from foreign intervention, and so we wanted to bring that conversation into Occupy.

Like many experienced activists, Prema had participated in anti-war activism in opposition to the Iraq War after September 11, 2001. She refused to abandon economic analysis about the military and war to focus solely on the banks, foreclosures, and economic crisis. Due to her consciousness about the economics of war along with her desire to build coalitions between Occupy and the anti-war movement, Prema created demonstrations with veterans on the periphery of OWS encampments. She describes one of these actions:

> We printed out the name of a country and the dates of U.S. intervention since the 1950s—one hundred of the places that the U.S. has done interventions. We stood in a half circle in front of Zuccotti Park. Each person was holding a sign, a black poster with white wording on it. Everybody was quiet. No one was saying anything. For silence, we had put either an American flag or a Chase Bank logo on the person's mouth. Chase Bank is connected to the military industry and corporations that pushed for the invasion of Iraq, and that's how we were trying to make the connection between anti-war and Occupy. . . . It was just very important to us, because a lot of us felt that the global picture was not a part of the 99%.

By demonstrating against Chase Bank's and the U.S. government's responsibility for U.S. military interventions, Prema and other anti-war protesters critiqued the Occupy movement and developed an anti-war oppositional collective identity within it. They argued that the 2008 financial crisis was only one contributor to economic inequality in the United States and globally. The group deployed the intersectional imperative to create an oppositional collective identity for experienced anti-war protesters, veterans, and people who analyzed the global dimensions of class inequality. Analysis of the military industrial complex was obscured within the Occupy movement and created a barrier to coalition building with anti-war movements. Groups like Prema's exposed the 99% as being composed of people from many different class identities and holding multiple analyses of economic inequality. While the overall loose structure of the Occupy movement allowed for peripheral protests, such as the anti-war demonstration, the main movement's organizations did not alter the 99% identity in response to anti-war or global critiques.

Despite the movement's framing as a place for everyone of all classes aside from the 1%, unacknowledged class diversity within the movement led to conflicts and tensions. For some participants, the 99% collective identity meant a movement with a large social-media aspect that was led by underemployed millennials. Alternatively, some participants saw the Occupy movement as a place to reveal their particular economic hardships, work experiences, and housing statuses. Class-based cleavages within Occupy and the broadness of the 99% identity became insufficient to describe the class diversity within the movement.

Conclusion

In the first issue of the *Post Post Script* zine (dated December 2011), participants in (un)Occupy encapsulated the difficulties of creating a mass movement:

> As this movement deepens and people bring the arduous task of really listening to each other, the question of who "we" are, both collectively and individually, is nuanced, complex, contentious. Yet we believe contention is not a divisive and destructive force, and is instead one that propels us to expand our understanding of ourselves, and each other, and to enrich our commitment to transforming our relationships both within and beyond our movement.

Represented by the "(un)" in its name, (un)Occupy formed in opposition to the main movement's collective identity. Similar to the opposition raised by the Decolonize movement, it opposed the lack of consciousness about race and gender politics in the main movement's organizations. The *Post Post Script* zine amplified critiques of the movement based on intersectional analyses. Groups of activists constantly deliberated questions: Who are the 99%? What does it mean to be a part of Occupy? What is the extent of our solidarity with each other? Deciding how to come together was a difficult, conflict-filled process.

By framing the movement's collective identity as "We are the 99%," Occupy leaders and participants sought to generate broad inclusivity by creating a boundary between only the richest 1% and everyone else. The 99% identity electrified the early days of the movement and encouraged experienced activists and ordinary persons to come to their town squares, share their grievances, and contribute to demonstrations for change. They embraced solidarity based on not being part of the 1%. The movement's focus on economic justice encouraged many diverse people to join it.

However, many participants were conscious about more than just class inequality. Experienced activists from anti-racist, feminist, LGBTQ, homeless, student, and anti-war movements wanted recognition of their particular identities and to form coalitions with other movements' organizations. These participants set new boundaries and developed new practices to reflect their consciousness about the race, gender, and sexual dimensions of class inequalities. Despite infighting about the Occupy movement's collective identity, most of these participants did not abandon Occupy completely; instead, many developed intersectional oppositional collective identities that brought together the Occupy identity and identities generated from intersectional analysis. Marginalized persons shifted their work into collectivities that better represented their identities, grievances, and interests for coalition building. Yet conflicts about the 99% identity were not met with expansive listening and collaboration by participants in the main movement's organizations or participants who continued to rely on monist analyses of class. As a result, Occupy fragmented into a variety of loosely connected groups, each with its own oppositional collective identity.

Across race, gender, sexuality, and class-based oppositional collective identities, social media was transformational to forming the new subgroups. Participants used Facebook, Twitter, blog posts, and email lists to air their conflicts with the main movement's organizations. They amplified their voices online, and their grievances quickly became collective through social media. Social media was a new and important tool for developing oppositional consciousness and then quickly publicizing meetings and protests where individuals could act on that consciousness. When oppositional groups mobilized, they specifically included people with experience in other movements (e.g., racial-justice activists, feminists, students, and antiwar activists). These new groups shifted support away from the main movement's events and organizations. I argue that they employed the intersectional imperative, while the main movement's organizations did not respond systematically to conflicts and fragmentation. Being specific about who was included and the intention to form coalitions with other movements contributed to solidarity within the oppositional groups.

Oppositional collective identities form within social movements so that individuals can act on their feelings of exclusion and grievances unacknowledged by the main groups. A new group may break away to pursue a related or alternative goal for social change. They can develop innovative tactics ignored by or unfeasible for the larger social movement. Activists form oppositional collective identities to create inclusivity and solidarity with otherwise marginalized participants. Although many of the debates about identity in Occupy were submerged within the movement and rarely visible to the media, the vibrancy and momentum of Occupy were a result of not only those subscribing to the 99% identity but also participants in the many oppositional groups. Tensions about collective identity enlivened the mass movement.

However, activists squandered much of the vibrant energy and debate around intersectionality within the Occupy movement. When conflicts arise and groups decide to break away into oppositional collective identities, it is time for the main movement's organizations to respond—even if that response requires pausing the development of the public-facing movement. Critiques that motivate marginalized participants to create separate organizations should be a signal for

leaders within the main movement to address concerns about intersectionality, diversity, and inclusivity within their internal dynamics.
Rather than accept the siphoning of volunteers into separate groups,
activists must adjust the boundaries of the main movement's organizations to be inclusive of oppositional collective identities. Adjusting
a movement's collective identity to address infighting is an arduous
process, but it can be productive for expanding an entire movement
(Ghaziani 2008). Yet, in the case of the Occupy movement, separate
oppositional groups became only loosely connected to the main
movement, and infighting was not addressed comprehensively, which
led to splits, fissures, and the movement's decline.

"Sorry for the Mess.
New Paradigm Under Construction"

*Inclusivity Frames in the Movement's
Media and Culture*

P articipants from a range of Occupy Wall Street (OWS) and Occupy Oakland (OO) working groups[1] created traditional and
new social media to support the movement. They produced
newspapers, radio shows, and YouTube channels. They passed out
flyers and pamphlets face-to-face at protests. They spread information online using discussion forums and websites. Just some of the art
that supported the movement included signs, posters, music recordings, songbooks, banners, videos, buttons, T-shirts, and photographs
(for more specific information about the media and cultural products
included in this study, see the Methodological Appendix). The Occupy movement embraced one of the most basic and fundamental
values of American culture and the internet: freedom of speech. Anyone could create citizen journalism, write a blog, or produce a video
about the Occupy mobilizations.

To support the movement's protest encampments, a couple of men
created a video. Soft music plays in the background as the camera
pans an Occupy encampment, pausing on close-ups of women laugh-
ing, baring their midriffs and cleavage, and tossing their hair. The
filmmakers interviewed a few of the women, but others they depicted
like models during a fashion shoot. As a companion to the video, the

filmmakers created a website featuring photos of the female activists and encouraged visitors to "like" or vote for their favorite.

The video and website, "Hot Chicks of Occupy Wall Street,"[2] became the subject of intense debate about the movement's media, culture, strategies, and gender dynamics (McVeigh 2011). Some participants defended the filmmakers, arguing that anyone could develop any kind of media that would publicize the movement. They reasoned that Occupy was a movement with a decentralized leadership structure, which relied on a large, unregulated volunteer network. With a lot of leeway regarding content and political correctness, Occupy participants supported a range of cultural expressions to reflect the movement's diversity. Some supporters of this view recognized "Hot Chicks" as a gorgeous portrayal of women's activism. This video brought significant attention to the protest encampments, and, as a by-product, it and the accompanying website became tools for the recruitment of heterosexual men to the protests.

On the other hand, feminists argued that the "Hot Chicks" website likened women to chickens and sexual objects, portraying them as token activists. Feminists criticized the video for featuring primarily thin, young, white women or light-skinned women of color. They argued that the images conformed to gendered, racial, and sexual stereotypes, limiting who counted as beautiful or as legitimate activists. They also suggested that the video and website actually discouraged the participation of women and feminists, especially women of color.

In the encampments and online, participants debated about whether to acknowledge "Hot Chicks" as a contribution to the Occupy movement or to demand that the filmmakers shut down the site. The website and video triggered extensive discussion online about sexism in the media and in social movements. Even the filmmakers acknowledged the controversy, arguing, "Create constructive discussions about the issues you have [with the video]. Because, to be honest, any excuse is a good excuse to bring up the topic of women's rights." In response to the "Hot Chicks" media and other sexist cultural products created by chauvinist male activists—or "mactivists,"[3] as some participants labeled them—cisgender and trans women initiated feminist organizations and protests. They networked with established feminist organizations from outside the Occupy movement to address sexist media about the Occupy activists. They also created their own feminist frames, slogans, flyers, and blogs specific to the Occupy mobilizations, including "Feminist General Assembly" (FemGA) town-hall meetings. FemGA demonstrations targeted sexism and racism within the Occupy movement and in society broadly.

While activists invited 99% of people to participate in the movement, the culture created by some of the participants alienated others. While organizing a massive, decentralized, largely online social movement, most Occupy activists could not—or would not—regulate the media and culture created about it. Free-speech advocates and advocates for a diverse mass movement argued that to create widespread radical change, a social movement needs a large number of diverse people, and participants will create change in many different ways. Yet the controversy over the "Hot Chicks" website is one example of the challenges that Occupy activists confronted as they sought to frame the culture and media of the mass movement. The creators of the "Hot Chicks" website characterized the meaning of inclusivity and exclusivity of the movement in particular ways. Their portrayal of young, conventionally feminine, traditionally sexually appealing, mostly white women activists signaled that the movement was a place for these types of women or for heterosexual men attracted to these women—to the exclusion of anyone else.

Inclusivity Frames: Conveying the Meanings of Intersectional Praxis

"Hot Chicks" is one example of how Occupy leaders, the rank and file, and supporters created media and culture to convey particular messages about the movement. They used words and symbols to describe, or "frame," the meanings of their protests, and they conveyed their grievances, goals, and group identity to mobilize collective action (Snow 2004; Taylor and Whittier 1992). Through language and artistic interpretations of a movement, its activists negotiate its defining features. By engaging in "frame alignment processes," they modify the frames to motivate volunteers. The media either reinforce the frames created by movement participants or challenge the activists' framing by developing counterframes, which may motivate activists to revise their frames again (Benford and Snow 2000). A movement's targets also evaluate these frames to find ways to stifle its momentum. As participants create media and cultural products, they are constantly presenting interpretations of a mass movement as being exclusive or inclusive. I evaluate the frames within the Occupy movement's media and cultural products intersectionally to address the following questions: How do gender, race, class, and sexuality processes influence contemporary social movements' dynamics and cultures? And under what conditions do movements' cultures exclude or alienate particular individuals and groups?

In addition to a movement's objectives, frames convey a basis for solidarity. Occupy participants constructed distinct meanings about who should be included or excluded. They represented these meanings discursively and symbolically in the movement's media and cultural products. Cultural products and media are some of many ways in which activists "negotiate" or continually construct a movement's collective identity (Taylor and Whittier 1992). "Inclusivity frames" are kinds of collective-action frames that convey a movement's basis for solidarity. They symbolize the "we" of a movement: who is welcome and included in its organizations. They also often depict the "them" of a movement: who is unwelcome, unnecessary to the goals for social change, or the enemy. This chapter examines three different inclusivity frames that Occupy activists used to signal who to encompass in the mass movement. Each kind of inclusivity frame indicates to what extent participants determined a basis for solidarity by engaging in intersectional praxis.

First, some Occupy-produced media celebrated the 99% identity and encouraged anyone except the wealthiest 1% of people to join. These cultural products and practices signaled for solidarity among nearly everyone according to their economic standing but left open for interpretation who was specifically included or represented. This "99% frame" did not represent an intersectional analysis; instead, it was a universalist frame that characterized solidarity by using a monist analysis of class. Like flawed feminist frames that lump all women into one universal collective without recognizing the many differences among them (Carastathis 2016; Lépinard 2007; Young 1997), the 99% frame fell short of specifically detailing activists' experiences of inequalities related to gender, race, or sexuality. As a result, it tended to exclude more vulnerable and multiply marginalized groups, which explained their experiences of oppression as a consequence of not only class inequality but also race, gender, and other structures of inequality.

The second inclusivity frame utilized symbols from the dominant American cultures of whiteness and masculinity. Media and cultural products that engaged a "dominance frame" symbolized the Occupy movement as powerful, a force to be feared, and sometimes violent. Media using the dominance fame conveyed support for aggressive masculinity and whiteness, while portraying the absence of femininity, queerness, and nonwhite cultures. As its name suggests, the frame did not examine multiple forms of inequality but reflected the stories of people from dominant groups. Media and cultural products that used the dominance frame often aggressively critiqued the 1%. However, they did not represent the movement's collective identity as a diverse "we" fitting for a mass movement of 99% of the people; instead, they suggested that a very specific group of aggressive, usually white, often male protesters were the most necessary participants.

Finally, some media and cultural practices specifically reflected the inclusion of women and genderqueer persons of a range of racial and ethnic identities, people of color of various genders, lesbian and gay participants, people of differing abilities and disabilities, indigenous people, and immigrants. This type of media deployed an "intersectional frame," signaling solidarity among people of multiple and marginalized identities. In addition, by representing and thereby valuing their specific identities, it called multiply marginalized persons to act (Bernstein 2008; Terriquez 2015). Each of these media and cultural products examined economic inequality as a result of not only class-based structures but also racialized and/or gendered distributions of power. As activists developed intersectional analyses and represented them by using intersectional frames, they created intersectional praxis (Townsend-Bell 2011).

Only media and cultural products that used the intersectional frame fulfilled the intersectional imperative. These media and cultural products symbolized specifically multiple forms of inequality, depicted the lives and stories of people who were multiply marginalized, and encouraged coalition building. When Occupy participants created cultural products and media that specifically represented people who endure multiple forms of inequality, they signaled inclusivity beyond white men. By representing a wider range of experiences, these media and cultural products framed the collective identity of the movement as diverse. Using an intersectional frame, media and cultural practices signaled support for the Occupy movement *and* feminist, transgender rights, civil rights, lesbian and gay, and/or other social movements seeking to end forms of inequality and discrimination. The extent to which participants framed media and cultural products to prioritize or exclude particular groups sparked debate and divisions within the broader Occupy movement.

"All Roads Lead to Wall Street": The Opportunities and Limits of the 99% Frame

Wielding fat-tipped markers, participants scrawled the title of this chapter, "Sorry for the Mess. New Paradigm under Construction," on the backs of empty cardboard pizza boxes. Protesters held the signs and propped them up as decorations around the encampments. During the first days of the occupations, some participants threw them down and slept on top of them. In 2011, as members of the first widespread social movement to use Facebook extensively for organizing and recruitment, Occupiers posted pictures of protesters holding their signs. Slogans like "Sorry for the Mess. New Paradigm under Construction," "We are the 99%," "Looking for a better world," "Shit is fucked up and Bullshit," "People over profits!" and even "Wake up!" conveyed an open-ended inclusivity. They framed many messages around the idea that anyone who felt disgruntled and wanted a new kind of social change was welcome—as long as they were not hoarding money and assets as part of the wealthiest 1% of the population.

Throughout this study, I found cultural products and media that framed inclusivity as the 99% indicated that nearly everyone was included—but no one specifically. This 99% frame provided an opportunity for activists to create a hodgepodge of cultural products and online media. The 99% identity was messy, sometimes chaotic, supportive of major economic change, and open to anyone's interpretation. It encouraged the movement's supporters to "do whatever you want."

Often participants used the 99% frame to represent the movement as a space for people of many different identities. For example, the

October 22, 2011, issue of the *Occupied Wall Street Journal* featured a series of separate photographs of participants holding whiteboards. In each photo, the participant reveals a reason for being part of the 99%. A veteran in fatigues, a young woman wearing a head scarf, a black man with cornrows, a Wall Street worker, and a young woman with blond hair each hold a dry-erase board on which they have written a personal testimony ending with the words "I am the 99%." The veteran's board reads, "We didn't land on Wall St., Wall St. landed on Us! I am the 99%." Here, the 99% framing provided participants an opportunity to express their unique grievances against economic injustice, yet the whiteboard campaign did not call for coalition building with other social movements or for fighting inequalities beyond economic injustice.

Artists, musicians, and activists amplified the Occupy movement's 99% frame. For instance, Marion, a white musician and activist since the 1960s, participated in the Zuccotti Park encampment and spent some of his time there photographing creative signs. Later, he used the photographs and slogans to create protest songs to support the movement:

> One of my favorite signs was "Stop using the mainstream press as an excuse for your apathy." I was like, "Oh yeah, that's right, that's exactly what I do every time I read the paper." One of my favorite ones more recently was "Forget the signs, it's time for action." Here's another one: "Lost my job but I found an occupation." . . . It's hard to say that you could make a unified statement, although they did in late September come out with little pamphlets, "The Declaration of the Occupation," so to some extent, this is what people consented to being a part of.

Like many Occupy supporters, Marion appreciated the perceptive, cheeky slogans on signs at the encampments. They endeared him to the demonstrations, and the messages inspired him to create singalongs. Yet he also conveyed some uneasiness about whether these messages, or even "The Declaration of the Occupation of New York City" pamphlet, really signaled a unifying movement. The text that begins "The Declaration" is illuminating:

We the people, acknowledge the reality: that the future of the human race requires the cooperation of its members; that our system must protect our rights, and upon corruption of that system, it is up to individuals to protect their own rights, and those of their neighbors . . .

Exemplary of the 99% frame, "The Declaration" argues that all individuals have equal responsibility to create change alongside the whole of the human race. It does not acknowledge the particular hardships or unique contributions of women, people of color, queer people, or anyone else. The statement's broadness is intended to convey inclusivity. Marion summarizes why he appreciated the broad 99% framing: "Occupy was a way to rephrase everything I already knew. Even anybody who wasn't in Occupy now talks about the 99%. It was a way of talking about who you are and who is the ultra-rich. It was a reframing that really worked." The message of class conflict between the "haves" and the "have-nots" resonated with Marion, but the 99% framing did not make him feel particularly represented within the movement. He also revealed that he showed up at encampments, drifted among different groups, and sang some songs, but he was not completely sure that he would even call himself an Occupier. In these examples, the 99% framing addressed only class inequality and did not reflect multiply marginalized individuals' life stories.

Many all-day protest encampments used the 99% framing to encourage broad participation and address many different grievances simultaneously. Exemplary was the "movement's birthday" on September 17, 2012, one year after its start. Occupy activists created celebratory protests in many places across the country, with the largest in New York City. Determined to keep up the momentum of the movement, activists gathered for nearly four full days of protests, workshops, and general assemblies. Organizers encouraged mass participation by framing the New York celebration with the slogan, "All Roads Lead to Wall Street." Interpreting "All Roads" as the opportunity to advocate for many different kinds of social change, participants transformed the "birthday party" into a wild carnival of activism. Some argued for the regulation of greedy big banks, some called for relief from student loans, and some demanded climate justice and protested the building of the Spectrum pipeline through green spaces and residential areas of Manhattan, and many other causes. Over email discussion lists and social media, organizers encouraged protesters to create small temporary "affinity groups." Affinity groups were groups of five to twenty protesters who created unique protest performances. The demonstration became a patchwork of all the different affinity groups' protests. A few of the dozens of affinity groups that participated included Youth Liberation Front (to address students' concerns), Occupy Faith (a coalition of religious leaders), and the Time's Up Polar Bears on Bikes (environmental activists). Even though individual protest performances were not driven by an intersectional analysis, taken as a whole, the affinity groups and the mass protests they created addressed several inequalities. Theoretically, anyone was welcome to participate however they wanted. People of marginalized or vulnerable identities were represented at the demonstration if they created an affinity group to represent their interests. Yet no centralized organizing hub orchestrated the affinity groups or checked to see who might be underrepresented. Furthermore, the protests advantaged more experienced, nondisabled activists without child care responsibilities, who could navigate the sometimes-chaotic days of action with many co-occurring meetings and demonstrations.

Cultural events and media that utilized a 99% frame allowed the majority of participants to avoid explicit discussions about sexism, racism, and other dimensions of power. Representative was the 2012 May Day march and rally hosted by Occupy Santa Barbara, which considered some economic grievances among Latinxs. The May Day protest called for support for driver's licenses for undocumented workers. The daylong protests ended with a citywide vigil for immigrants' rights. However, most of the promotional materials for the event focused on abstract class issues represented by such slogans as "Greed is not Good." The movement called for protesters to take action, bring food, march up the main street of the city, and "collaborate about our shared future goals for social, economic, and environmental justice." The protest included a range of issues and broadly addressed a variety of forms of inequality, yet it ultimately prioritized class issues and marginalized the immigrants' rights aspects of the day. Due in part to its 99% framing, the May Day calls for collaboration actually shifted the protest frame *away* from Latinxs' grievances. The protest defaulted to grievances about economic inequality in the abstract, thereby limiting opportunities to address the particular inequalities suffered by Latinx and undocumented persons.

More marginal, vulnerable, or oppressed populations could participate in cultural performances and media that used the 99% frame, but their grievances were likely to be subsumed under a broad banner for economic change. Therefore, particular experiences of multiply marginalized persons were likely to remain unseen within media or cultural events using the 99% frame. Angie Beeman (2015, 131) identifies the marginalization of race issues and/or the prioritization of class above racial inequalities as a "racism evasiveness strategy." In her study of an interracial social movement organization, she observed activists exercising white privilege and developing racist organizations when they did not recognize explicitly racial inequality. I argue that media and cultures that used the open-ended 99% framing did not acknowledge that the 2008 financial crisis disproportionately affected communities of color (Oliver 2008). Protesters often ignored the disproportionate number of foreclosures, unemployed workers, and loss of wealth among communities of color, and especially women of color. Without including gender or race specificity, the 99% framing contrasted strikingly with historic and recent inequalities in black communities, in other communities of color, and among women of color (National Association of Real Estate Brokers 2013; Oliver 2008; Oliver and Shapiro 2006). Such slogans and symbols as "Get money out of politics" or "They got bailed out, we got sold out" did not represent people of color's or women's distinct experiences and therefore conveyed exclusivity rather than inclusivity.

The Dominance Frame: Masculinity, Whiteness, and Power on Display

Charging Bull is a large metal statue near Wall Street in New York City's financial district. It symbolizes a "bull" market, lucrative stock prices, and profits for investors. Bulls also symbolize Wall Street values, such as aggressive capitalism and risk taking. In addition, bulls are male cows used for breeding and therefore have become a prized symbol of masculinity. Most of *Charging Bull* is bronze, but the bull's testicles have a golden gleam. Bringing together the ideas of financial success and praise for masculinity, people rub the bull's testicles for good luck.

As part of the original call to Occupy Wall Street, *Adbusters* magazine "culture jammed," or created an image to symbolically protest Wall Street. The image depicts a woman performing the ballet position "second arabesque" on top of *Charging Bull*. Her pose symbolizes how protests against Wall Street should follow in the tradition of protests from early 2011 in Tunisia, Egypt, and other Arab countries and aspire to become a second Arab Uprising. In the image, a fog of tear gas and ten protesters outfitted in black sweatshirts and gas masks surround *Charging Bull* and the dancer. Occupy protest participants and supporters frequently deployed the *Adbusters* image in flyers, posters, signs, T-shirts, and protest art spread online through memes on Facebook. Like many of the symbolic protests included in *Adbusters* (Wettergren 2005), the image of *Charging Bull*, the dancer, tear gas, and protesters critiques power holders while conveying an urgent need for change. The white, lithe, feminine dancer appears strong. She is in control on top of the statue. However, the image also re-inscribes an ideal of white, heterosexual beauty and femininity at the exclusion of fat bodies and people of color. Although the dancer symbolizes the movement as feminine in opposition to the masculine bull, the other protesters in the image are depicted as high-risk-taking, aggressive, likely masculine protesters who wear black hoodies and gas masks to demonstrations. Typically, protesters wear this type of clothing to indicate that they identify as "black bloc anarchists," who perform acts of civil disobedience. Many anarchist protesters joined and contributed greatly to the Occupy movement (Bray 2013; Gould-Wartofsky 2015; Schneider 2013). Protests that were heavily populated by anarchists, especially in Oakland, often replicated the scene in the poster. The poster symbolizes the people's power over the finance industry but also idolizes aggressive protesters.

Across many different forms of online and traditional media, Occupy participants modified the *Charging Bull* symbol to critique the financial industry. By appropriating the bull as a symbol of the Occupy movement, protesters also adopted the masculinity and aggression associated with it. Adaptations of the bull image include a poster printed on the back of the first issue of *Occupy! N+1 An OWS-Inspired*

Gazette that depicts a bull muzzled with a belt and the slogan "Money talks... too much. Occupy!" A pamphlet version of "The Declaration of the Occupation of New York City" includes the reproduction of a poster by Josh MacPhee of the Justseeds Artists' Cooperative suggestive of castrating the bull. The image features the backside of the bull marked with a dotted line, scissors above the bull's testicles, and the words "Cut This!" Several flyers portray bulls tied with thick ropes, struggling to get free. Protesters' distain for *Charging Bull* became so fierce that New York City police barricaded the actual statue for more than a year (Gillham, Edwards, and Noakes 2013). Protests that used the *Charging Bull* image critiqued the bull as a symbol of the financial industry but also appropriated the masculine aggression it conveyed.

In addition to images of *Charging Bull*, protesters developed other cultural products and practices to symbolize power and dominance. Some wore men's suits and masks to mock the 1%, government officials, and bankers. For example, they impersonated President Barack Obama and the banker from the Monopoly board game. They also satirized and demonized corporations. Exemplary was a six-foot-tall puppet inspired by the villain "Bane" from Batman comics. Artist and protester Gan Golan created the puppet to ridicule Massachusetts's governor Mitt Romney's company, Bain Capital. Media and cultural products that used the dominance frame usually reflected the actions of white, male, and/or heterosexual cultures rather than those of more vulnerable or marginalized populations.

By depicting the 1% as muscular, masculine, and powerful, media and cultural products reinforced the idea that white men are wealthy and dominant. Men and women in the Alternative Banking Working Group, part of OWS, coordinated a group of women and men artists to design an artistic deck of playing cards called "52 Shades of Greed." Each card is a stylized flashcard that critiques corporations and individuals responsible for the 2008 financial crisis. The group produced and distributed the decks to publicize harmful practices in the financial industry. For instance, each ace depicts a distinct "toxic institution," such as Goldman Sachs or Countrywide, and each five card displays a "toxic method," such as "leverage & looting."[4] The cards literally demonize such men as Jamie Dimon, the chief executive officer (CEO) of JPMorgan Chase and former chair of the Federal Reserve Bank of New York, who is caricatured wearing a suit while coddling a skeleton and a safe full of money. Only the four queen cards and a sexualized image of a serpent on the "accounting tricks" card (the eight of diamonds) portray images of women; all the other images in the deck depict men, masculine monsters in suits, or objects. Furthermore, the name of the deck of cards is a twist on the title of the erotic novel *50 Shades of Grey*, a story about a wealthy white businessman's proclivity for sadomasochism and a woman's submission to him. The novel epitomizes the masculine leisure and erotica that are valued on Wall Street. "52 Shades of Greed" satirizes the title of the novel, drawing on its cultural resonance. Although the deck of cards ingeniously targets and critiques the financial industry, to create cultural resonance, the cards depict masculine images and reinforce the idea that finance is largely a male-dominated context.

Many media and cultural products produced by Occupiers celebrated an emotion culture of anger reflective of the experiences of white men. For example, *The Debt Resistors' Operations Manual*[5] explains student and medical debt and bankruptcy. It suggests strategies for disputing banks about debt and dealing with credit fraud. Women and men wrote and distributed the material. While the authors provide a wealth of research and information, the manual resonates with the cultures of the financial and banking industries. It draws on the emotion culture of rationality and traditionally masculine anger. The manual suggests that readers write "angry letters," because the information in the manual should have "made you angry." It also urges readers to transform shame about debt "into outrage—and that outrage into action" (Debt Resistors 2012, 102). The Debt Resistors argue for Occupy participants and adherents to accept and express their anger. However, the text ignores the gendered and raced consequences that all women—especially women of color—and men of color face when they express their anger in white male–dominated contexts, such as finance and banking. Elite white men may be rewarded for expressing anger (Blee 2002; Messner 1997), but women and racial minorities endure harsh punishments. They may face ostracism or be considered irrational. Beyond being discounted, women and minorities often suffer physical harm or even incarceration if they express anger rather than submission (Connell and Messerschmidt 2005; Rios 2011). Scholars R. W. Connell and James Messerschmidt (2005) suggest that anger and aggression are emotions representative of hegemonic masculinity, whereas most women's anger is considered deviant. When Occupiers created media and culture that drew on the emotion cultures of white men, they used a dominance frame rather than one that was inclusive of women and people of color.

Using the dominance frame, some protesters conveyed their serious desire to take power away from the 1%. Several of the movement's slogans advocated confrontation, such as, "Hungry? Eat a banker" or "Mass arrests prove our power." Slogans using the dominance frame emphasized risk taking, aggression, fighting, violence, or confrontations with the police, bankers, and corporations. In mid-2012, the "Fuck the Police" (FTP) movement grew out of a collaboration between Occupy participants, anarchists, and anti-police brutality protesters. The movement condemned police brutality by using aggressive language. Its participants advocated for competition as a strategy to stop repression. The group's pamphlet reads: "The police exist to protect capitalism and the rich. . . . Revolt!" FTP slogans, such as "Police protecting and serving the shit out of you!" and "You cannot evict an idea," critiqued police brutality and asserted that activists would pursue their goals despite police threats to forcibly clear the encampments. The majority of Occupy documents about the police portrayed police versus protester aggression.

To legitimately and credibly target the financial industry, Occupy protesters developed media, slogans, and culture that resonated with and drew on the preexisting culture of the finance and banking industries. To change a particular institution, a movement must create claims that resonate within that cultural context (Benford and Snow 2000; McCammon et al. 2007). The civil rights movement amplified black culture, black communities, and the black church (Morris 1986; Robnett 1997). Likewise, the culture of the entertainment industry has infused the Me Too and TIME's UP movements spearheaded by actresses who oppose sexual harassment, sexual assault, and the gender pay gap. However, for the Occupy movement, the dominance frame based on the culture of Wall Street became problematic. From the *Charging Bull* symbol to the value assigned to risk taking and aggression, the dominance frame within the Occupy movement mirrored the heavily male-dominated and white-supremacist cultures of the finance industry. Men hold a disproportionate number of investment banking, trading, and finance jobs and earn significantly higher salaries in these jobs than do women (Fisher 2012; L. Roth 2006). Even through the 1980s, the majority of women who worked on Wall Street were secretaries rather than traders (L. Roth 2006). Jobs in banking and finance are coded as masculine, exemplified by the high value placed on making skilled but risky investments (Porter 2005). Risk taking is considered dominant and valuable because it can yield high profits and is seen as a skill that men possess (Fisher 2012). Even the leisure activities for Wall Street's male finance and banking employees are notoriously hypermasculine. Such activities as drinking excessively, attending strip clubs, and purchasing the services of sex workers allow men to perform stereotypically masculine behavior. The male-dominated cultural experiences common among men on Wall Street emphasize men's heterosexual prowess through the commodification and objectification of women's sexuality. While Occupy protesters opposed the finance and banking industries, the movement worked in, used the language of, and interacted with the symbols and frames of the white male–dominated culture of Wall Street.

Coalition Building with the Intersectional Frame

In contrast to either the 99% frame or dominance frame, when participants created cultural products and media that specifically represented people who endure several forms of inequality, they signaled inclusivity in the movement beyond white men. By creating cultural practices and media with an intersectional frame, they readily worked across social movement boundaries and built coalitions. Using intersectional frames to portray people's many identities, these activists exemplified Anna Carastathis's (2016, 185) argument that "identities are potential coalitions . . . [and] grounds for solidarity that reach across and reveal differences within categories of identity." The power of the intersectional frame to build coalitions would later become evident in the more sustained and diverse Black Lives Matter movement.

Trayvon Martin was a black high school student, walking alone through a Florida neighborhood, wearing a hoodie, eating Skittles candy, when George Zimmerman killed him. Zimmerman, a member of the neighborhood watch group, wrongly suspected that Martin was a criminal when he was really just a student walking home (Bates 2018;

McNight 2012). In the summer of 2013, Alicia Garza, Opal Tometi, and Patrisse Cullors drew on their outrage about Martin's wrongful death and Zimmerman's acquittal and their love for black people to create Black Lives Matter, a movement that provided an intersectional analysis of the inequalities endured by black people. Although many communities had protested police brutality and violence for decades preceding the creation of the Black Lives Matter movement, these events had rarely received more than local media attention.

Prior to the emergence of Black Lives Matter, in the spring of 2012 experienced civil rights activists, the national InterOccupy network, people of color working groups within the Occupy movement, and activists opposed to police brutality and gun violence joined together to protest "stop-and-frisk" laws. The protests critiqued a policing tactic, now deemed unconstitutional, whereby police officers detained mainly black and Latinx persons without just cause on the streets of New York. Soon after protesting "stop and frisk," many of these same activists marched while wearing hooded sweatshirts, or "hoodies," to protest Martin's February 2012 death. Occupy participants and a range of civil rights and racial justice organizations mobilized hoodie marches to demand justice for Martin. Instead of working within the 99% frame or the dominance frame, participants conceived of inclusivity intersectionally in the "stop-and-frisk" protests and hoodie marches. They analyzed police violence as a combination of class and racial domination and gave particular voice to the experiences of black men. Furthermore, they designed these protests to build relationships between social movements—in this case, the Occupy movement, the anti–police brutality movement, the civil rights movement, and the gun control movement. The hoodie marches and anti-stop-and-frisk demonstrations are exemplary of a different kind of inclusivity. To develop culture and media that used an intersectional frame, Occupy participants often borrowed from other established social movements.

A variety of protests fulfilled the intersectional imperative by specifically identifying multiple forms of inequality, depicting the lives and stories of people who are multiply marginalized, and encouraging coalition building. For example, wearing tutus to impersonate the dancer on top of *Charging Bull* from the *Adbusters* call to action became a way to express support for the 99% while also signaling acceptance of femininity and of cross-dressing. Several gay but also a few heterosexual men and women supported Occupy by dressing up like ballerinas, wearing pink panties and/or skirts or dressing in drag. Russe Guy, a white gay man, explains the utility of cross-dressing during protests:

> During a protest, I'll use cross-dressing for the purposes of attention-getting. It's pretty cool, though—since I started it, I have gotten a lot of interesting and generally pretty positive reactions from people. On a personal level, it is pretty interesting to hear a guy say that you look hot in your bustier.

Participants who cross-dressed during protest events endorsed the 99% identity, strengthened the movement with their attention-getting participation, and challenged gender essentialism, the idea that anything feminine is only reserved for women's self-expression. The wearing of tutus or pink panties became an accepted cultural practice that represented the acceptance of feminine and queer participants; drew on and amplified lesbian, gay, bisexual, transgender, and queer/questioning (LGBTQ) movement practices; and, at the same time, brought attention to the 99% identity.

Cultural products and practices that critiqued the 1% and gender essentialism advocated for the acceptance of gender diversity while protesting class inequality. For example, men and women wore Guy Fawkes masks, a masculine, white face with thick black eyebrows, goatee, and mustache popularized in the 2005 movie *V for Vendetta* and by the Anonymous movement.[6] A few women participants "queered" the masks, adding feminine touches to the masculine features by painting makeup, rainbows, or glitter on the masks or wearing their long hair spilling over them. By mixing feminine and masculine characteristics, they mitigated the dominance frame and instead created an intersectional frame. Exemplary of gender bending and drawing on protest imagery from the Occupy and women's movements is artist Alexandra Fischer's poster depicting Rosie the Riveter wearing a Guy Fawkes mask. The poster calls for the 99% to shut down the West Coast ports and "Show your muscle!" Protest performances, cultural symbols, and media that combined traditionally masculine and feminine images to create queer representations deployed an intersectional frame. The protests supported Occupy, gender-nonconformity, feminism, and LGBTQ goals simultaneously.

Another cultural practice that participants developed to create awareness about gender diversity alongside class inequality was the use of Preferred Gender Pronouns[7] (PGPs). At the beginning of meetings and protest events, they instructed participants to introduce themselves with their names and the gender pronouns that they used to refer to themselves, such as she, he, or they. Genderqueer, transgender, and/or feminist participants and anyone else could state that they would like to be identified with a gender-neutral or genderqueer pronoun, such as "they." For example, at the start of a working group meeting where participants sat around a table, a facilitator might invite participants to get involved by saying, "To start this meeting, each person please introduce yourself, share your PGP, and let us know what you would like to discuss today." In turn, each participant would divulge, "Hi, my name is Jasmine, I prefer she or her, and I am here to help plan the May Day rally" or "My name is Andre, I prefer they, and I think we need to spend some time tonight making posters for the march this coming weekend." There was neither a standard training about how to use gender pronouns nor a requirement to include the cultural practice. Participants who identified themselves as feminist or genderqueer typically introduced it during meetings and events. Rebecca explains how she brought gender pronouns into her theater group's performance to support Occupy and gender nonconformity:

> We did this show called *Jack and the Corporate Beanstalk* where Jack was played by a woman. Whereas the traditional Jack would go by "he," in our modern retelling of this fairy tale, we could not decide Jack's gender, so for the most part, we would say Jack's preferred gender pronoun is "Jack."

In *Jack and the Corporate Beanstalk*, activists chose to portray the lead as a gender-nonconforming person. In the story, Jack goes to college to find a job and magic beans but encounters a greedy Corporate Giant from whom Jack has to take back the Golden Goose for the 99%. The actors portrayed the hero of the 99%, Jack, as having a third gender identity—"Jack"—rather than identifying as a woman or man. Like the lesbian and gay movements' "coming-out" strategies that take pride in sexual diversity (Whittier 2012), the use of gender pronouns enabled participants to "come out" to express their gender identity. Activists transformed language about gender to accept people of all gender identities. Contributing to the movement's prefigurative world, activists used the gender pronouns tactic to challenge the gender binary; even while protesting for economic justice, they embraced gender diversity beyond "she" and "he." Although the practice was common in contemporary feminist and transgender rights organizations in the 2010s, many activists first learned about using gender pronouns during Occupy protests.

In addition to transforming the movement's language to recognize inequalities intersectionally, some participants challenged narrowly defined gender expectations for fashion. Sam, a young woman of color in the hundred-plus-degree heat at the Occupy National Gathering (NatGat), removed her shirt and wore rectangular "I ♥ the 99%" stickers over her nipples, dubbing the practice "occupasties." Five other men and women joined in. Sam wanted to challenge stereotypically feminine ways of dressing that suggested that men were allowed to take off their shirts but women were not. For her, occupasties symbolized human rights and equality. She explained that the action allowed her to advocate for gender equality while supporting the 99%. Likewise, Saige, another woman NatGat attendee, explains, "I was really surprised at how comfortable I felt being shirtless in that environment, because I am usually not even comfortable being shirtless around someone that I'm intimate with, and so it was very liberating for me." Sam and Saige were like the small but highly visible number of women at Occupy protests in New York, the San Francisco Bay Area, New Orleans, and NatGat who sought to transform the prefigurative culture of the movement by removing their shirts, stripping, or performing burlesque dances to support the movement. Each of these cultural practices united support for Occupy with advocacy for women's empowerment and queer, feminist, gender nonconformity. Although a few men ogled and sexualized the women, topless women in the Occupy movement channeled the attention they gained by removing their shirts to protest the 1%. They supported a gender-equal prefigurative society and the acceptance of women's bodies. Topless protests and occupasties borrowed from tactical repertoires used by members of the European feminist group FEMEN, which shames international leaders and draws attention to human-rights issues by disrobing during global justice protests. The wearing of occupasties created an intersectional frame for the encampment, encouraging a space for feminist, queer, and gender-bending expressions as part of a prefigurative society where women were safe and respected enough to be naked in public without being harassed.

Exemplary of culture and media that addressed economic justice, gender equality, and the specific needs of women participants was Occupy Denver's "Fishbowl Caucus" event. During the cultural performance, women and transgender persons formed an inner circle and "spoke bitterness"—in other words, they condemned the harassment and inequality they faced in the Occupy movement and in Denver in general. Men listened from an outer circle to learn from women and transgender participants' experiences. Similarly, Occupy Santa Barbara held a consciousness-raising session about personal space and argued against the sexualization of women in the movement. Participants offered training about the sexist double standard that expects men to greet strangers with handshakes and women to greet strangers, including men, with hugs. The group created an intersectional frame by enforcing a "politics of consent" within the group whereby even friends asked each other whether they would like to hug or just shake hands rather than assume that a woman would like to press her body against someone else's. Through such feminist rituals as the Fishbowl Caucus and the consciousness-raising session, Occupy participants created intersectional frames within which to explicitly discuss sexism and gender essentialism while mobilizing against class and gender inequality. By adopting the cultural practices of feminist and LGBTQ movements, Occupy participants created an intersectional frame with which to lay the groundwork for coalition building.

When Occupy participants used an intersectional frame for cultural products, artistic actions, and the movement's language and symbols, they created an atmosphere of inclusivity that extended beyond white men. Using the open and loose structure of the movement to frame culture and media intersectionally, they contributed to transforming gender, race, and sexual inequalities within and beyond the movement. Media and culture that deployed an intersectional frame recognized specifically individuals who endure class-based injustice and other oppressions simultaneously. While culture and media with an intersectional frame supported Occupy's goals by stimulating participation, these products also drew on and urged coalition building with LGBTQ, feminist, and racial justice movements.

Conclusion

The media and cultural products created by Occupy participants captivated the U.S. public. In words and symbols, participants framed the meanings of their protests to convey their grievances, goals, and who was included in the movement. The movement's messages transformed the national discussion about economic inequality, leading the idea of the 99% versus the 1% to become commonplace (Gaby and Caren 2016).

How to frame inclusivity within the Occupy movement was a topic of constant debate. The movement utilized media and culture that reproduced the objectification of women's bodies, such as the "Hot Chicks of Occupy Wall Street" video and website; advocated for the creation of a "New Paradigm"; celebrated hypermasculinity with images of *Charging Bull*; *and* shifted language toward the use of gender pronouns and the recognition of genders beyond just "male" and "female." Individuals developed the movement's frames through decentralized social media, within the main movement, and within groups that created oppositional collective identities. The myriad inclusivity frames mirrored the carnival-like, chaotic atmosphere within the Occupy movement in the streets and online. The variability of the movement's media and culture resulted from lack of oversight from an overarching committee.

Media and cultural practices were intended to encourage massive participation, and they did for a brief time in the fall of 2011. However, the diversity of activists required to create and sustain a mass movement was not adequately represented in media and culture framed by the 99% frame and the dominance frame.

The 99% frame was the most utilized inclusivity frame because of the remarkable idea of "the 99% versus the 1%." This frame also characterized the loose leadership structure and porous nature of the encampments and online spaces. Creating media and cultural practices with the 99% frame sometimes allowed individuals or groups to express multiple grievances simultaneously, such as during all-day encampments like the September 2012 birthday party. Yet the 99% frame also ignored the particular experiences of people of color, women, genderqueer persons, and sexual minorities.

The dominance frame prioritized the images and stories of privileged white masculinity. In addition, it reproduced the cultures of Wall Street. Neither the 99% frame nor the dominance frame elaborated meanings about the lives or grievances of women and queer persons of a variety of racial/ethnic backgrounds or men of color.

Only media and culture that used the intersectional frame allowed Occupy movement participants to combine their concerns for class, gender, sexual, racial, and other forms of inequality. Participants who represented inequalities intersectionally created media and culture that accomplished the intersectional imperative. When participants framed the movement's messages as not only being about Occupy or class inequality, they provided opportunities to build coalitions with participants from other contemporary movements.

Occupy activists developed media and culture that became a foundation for the contemporary protest wave. Evaluating inclusivity frames allows us to address these questions: Under what conditions do movement cultures exclude or alienate particular individuals and groups? How do gender, race, class, and sexuality processes influence contemporary social movement dynamics and culture?

Analysis of the Occupy movement's media and culture suggests several lessons for future social movements. Universalist frames that only vaguely call for solidarity across gender, race, class, and sexual identities do not signal to more marginalized participants that a movement is a welcoming and safe space for their participation and leadership. It will behoove participants in future social movements to not only establish committees that specialize in media development but work with participants to use intersectional praxis as they create citizen journalism, videos, and websites about their movements. Leaders of future movements should respond to media that convey a 99% frame or dominance frame and advocate for the development of intersectional frames. Framing identities and movements as intersectional signals an opportunity for coalition building (Carastathis 2013, 2016). The intersectional frame offers the most opportunities for building solidarity among people with diverse gender, race, class, and sexual identities.

Citizen journalism and the outpouring of diverse media created by unregulated volunteers, especially on social media, sparked great interest in the Occupy movement. However, some frames created divisions within the movement. Future movements may endure if activists find ways to stimulate voluntary media and culture production as well as guide the movements' messages toward the intersectional imperative. To do so, movements will need diverse leadership who play a more significant role than voluntary and rotating participants.

Discriminatory Resistance

*Gender and Race Dynamics
in a Leaderless Movement*

I n the second issue of the *Occupy N+1* newspaper, Astra Taylor describes a scene at Occupy Wall Street (OWS) where participants did not initially accept a woman's recommendation for the encampment:

> [A woman] was submitting a proposal to buy fifteen walkie-talkies . . . to communicate to keep things safe for everyone. . . . [T]here had been reports of fights, drug dealing, theft, and, finally, sexual harassment. . . . The crowd, however, seemed reluctant to believe these were serious issues until a young fellow from [the] sanitation [committee] stepped forward [and said], . . . "It's happening."

The crowd questioned this woman's claim that walkie-talkies were a necessary purchase until a man corroborated her view. Participants responded positively to the man after questioning the woman's credibility, even though both were advocating for the same proposal. These reactions suggest that the participants held gendered stereotypes about leadership. This episode illustrates followers' tendency toward "discriminatory resistance."[1] Discriminatory resistance

An earlier version of Chapter 3 was previously published as Hurwitz, Heather McKee. 2019. "Gender and Race in the Occupy Movement: Relational Leadership and Discriminatory Resistance." *Mobilization: An International Quarterly.*

constrained the woman's ability to make a decision and direct the activities of the encampment, recalling the experiences of women leaders on corporate boards whose ideas meet resistance until they are expressed by men (Eagly and Carli 2007; Kramer, Conrad, and Erkut 2006; Sandberg and Grant 2015). By doubting women's decision making, those participants who should have been following the woman leader's suggestions enacted gendered stereotypes about women's inability to lead and men's authority as appropriate.

When leaders or followers replicate patterns of inequality, they undermine the possibility for the intersectional imperative. Instead, they engage in practices within the leadership structure of social movements that perpetuate the privileging of certain people over others. They fail to appreciate leadership as being shaped by multiple and interlaced structures of inequality, which then inhibits the development of diverse leadership (P. Collins and Bilge 2016). Using both gender and racial stereotypes, followers diminish women and genderqueer persons of color's leadership. Discriminatory resistance limits who can lead social movements, often preventing leadership by minorities.

In addition to the walkie-talkie incident, Occupy participants engaged in several other acts of discriminatory resistance. This chapter reveals a framework for identifying this type of behavior. When followers perform discriminatory resistance, they impede leaders' work by acting implicitly or explicitly on racial and gendered prejudices. In the process, they perpetuate structures of inequality that privilege white male leaders.

If followers are guided by stereotypical beliefs about men being ideal leaders, they devalue women and genderqueer leaders. Likewise, followers' stereotypical beliefs about white persons as ideal leaders marginalize leaders of color. Followers choose how to interact with leaders based on their cultural beliefs about leaders' status (Ridgeway 2011). As followers evaluate leaders' authority, they are also evaluating simultaneously whether leaders fulfill cultural expectations about being a woman or man of a particular ethnic/racial identity (Ridgeway 2011; West and Zimmerman 1987). In this chapter, I show that Occupy followers frequently fell back on gender and racial stereotypes about white men as ideal leaders.

I analyzed leadership within the main movement's organizations and in groups with oppositional collective identities that had formed

in part to create leadership opportunities for marginalized participants. The analysis revealed structures of inequality that allowed people of particular social locations to fulfill leadership responsibilities.
This chapter focuses on the gender and raced dimensions of leadership to reveal the interactional process of discriminatory resistance.
Using discriminatory resistance, participants opposed the creation
of a diverse group of leaders. Stereotypes around who were the ideal
leaders created barriers to prefigurative politics. Whenever followers
engaged in discriminatory resistance, they precluded the development
of intersectional praxis.

Occupy movement participants aimed to allow anyone to be a
leader and thereby foster diverse leadership. However, the walkie-
talkie episode is one of many examples of participants sometimes
subtly, sometimes overtly, undermining that goal. By examining the
moments when participants fell back on sexist and racist discriminatory resistance, I show how the movement did not implement intersectional praxis. I address these research questions: Under what
conditions do movement cultures exclude or alienate particular
individuals and groups? How do gender, race, class, and sexuality
processes influence contemporary social movement dynamics and
culture? Discriminatory resistance is a recurring problem for women
leaders in workplaces and institutionalized politics (Eagly and Carli
2007), but in this chapter, I show how discriminatory resistance also
influenced leadership dynamics in a purportedly nonhierarchical
contemporary mass social movement.

Leadership Dynamics

A social movement's ability to meet its goals may depend in part on
how its leaders and followers interact with each other. When a social
movement's leaders direct protesters during marches or make decisions during meetings, their followers choose to accept and validate
or oppose and ignore them. Leaders take on the additional responsibilities of speaking, making decisions, or developing strategies within
a movement. They influence a social movement's progress by guid-
ing participants through decision-making processes about the organization and directing them in protests. At the same time, leaders
can only accomplish their work in concert with followers. Followers

listen, react, and offer support—or not. They interact with leaders to validate, accept, ignore, or oppose their directions.

The "leaderless" Occupy movement had a particularly active and diverse organization of followers and leaders. Its members mobilized in part by borrowing personnel, protest tactics, and "horizontal," or nonhierarchical, leadership strategies from earlier waves of participatory democracy, global justice, and anarchist movements (Bray 2013; Hammond 2015; Polletta and Hoban 2016; Sitrin 2012a, 2012b; J. Smith and Glidden 2012). In each local Occupy movement, participants volunteered for small, autonomous, nonhierarchical committees, or "working groups." In these working groups, participants volunteered for "bottom-liner" positions: temporary and rotating positions to lead actions, protests, and events. They also volunteered for "facilitator" positions, a term for bottom-lining meetings. Facilitating duties included running meetings, managing speakers, and leading decision-making procedures. In any particular meeting or protest, people who were not bottom-liners or facilitators possessed somewhat less authority and influence. While they were general active participants, they were also kinds of followers. Still, none of the individuals who performed leadership or followership roles held official titles. The Occupy movement's loose, rotating, and voluntary leadership structure provided an opportunity to observe a range of different leadership interactions, which are usually obscured by official titles or roles for leaders and followers in more bureaucratic organizations.

Occupy participants described the movement as allowing everyone to be a leader. However, not everyone led every meeting or action. Although it sometimes carries negative connotations, throughout this chapter, I use the term "follower" to distinguish individuals who are not taking on leadership responsibility in a particular moment or context and to engage in the conventions of public knowledge and scholarly work about leadership broadly. But instead of perpetuating stereotypes about followers, I define them as individuals who are agentic actors who contribute to leadership and all aspects of social movements. Followers and leaders hold each other accountable to expectations about who should lead, how they should do so, and the appropriate gender and race expressions they should demonstrate. Leadership is a socially constructed process (DeRue and Ashford 2010); without followers, there would be no one for leaders to lead.

Feminist Analysis of Leadership Stratification

Feminist scholars have begun to theorize how leaders of social movements, and sometimes followers, contribute to racialized gendered leadership stratification in social movements. Research about the underrepresentation of women in social movements' leadership positions recognizes that men leaders have denied women these opportunities in a range of movements, from the civil rights movement (Goss 2017) to conservative movements (Rohlinger and Claxton 2017). Sara Evans's (1979, 162) analysis of the New Left movement reveals how mostly male leaders and some followers stifled women's leadership with tactics ranging from booing and hissing to men using "jargon, verbal competitiveness, wrangling, and posturing." Women in the New Left movement endured social and psychological effects as well; confident women who attempted to take on leadership roles were seen by men "as threats[,] and they found themselves becoming overly conscious of such male reactions" (166). Also, Benita Roth (2004) documents how white activists and the media devalued Chicana and black women's leadership activities in 1960s' and 1970s' feminist movements. In response, feminists developed friendlier contexts in which to lead—namely, racially segregated women's movements. More recently, in her study of social justice groups that addressed Hurricane Katrina disaster relief in New Orleans, Rachel Luft (2016) finds that male leaders accepted figurehead leadership positions and accomplished ideological strategizing but refused to do the hard work of working phone banks, distributing flyers, and performing other grassroots leadership tasks, which fell to women. However, these women recognized the traditional gendered leadership stratification—men as formal leaders, women as underrecognized grassroots leaders—as sexist, and many left the movement. The Occupy movement provides a new contemporary opportunity to examine the gendered, racial, and intersectional dynamics of leadership.

The underrepresentation of women in leadership positions hinges on widely held cultural beliefs that women and men are different; therefore, followers hold them to expectations based on gendered stereotypes. While masculinity is stereotyped as agentic and aggressive (Connell 2005), femininity and leadership are often stereotyped in contradictory ways. Followers expect women leaders to act feminine, but not *too* feminine, and decisive, but not *too* bossy, a double standard known as the "double bind" (Eagly and Carli 2007). Victoria Brescoll (2016, 425) argues that women walk an emotional "tightrope." Their behavior must be appropriately feminine (caring, expressive, soft, nurturing, quiet, and kind) and, at the same time, appropriate for authoritative leaders (aggressive, rational/unexpressive, firm, hard, assertive, loud, and decisive). Followers are reticent to accept women chief executive officers (CEOs) as authentic, because they view women as outsiders in male-dominated spaces and positions. While a male CEO is considered an authentic leader for being confident and agentic, a female CEO is penalized in the media when she acts decisively but is accepted when she acts warm, friendly, caring, and passive (Liu, Cutcher, and Grant 2015). I argue that when followers believe that women leaders are being too feminine, not feminine enough, too aggressive, or not agentic enough, they create discriminatory resistance to impede women from becoming leaders or completing leadership tasks.

Women leaders must contend not only with followers' stereotypes but also with challenges to their authority and incivilities from followers, or what Alice Eagly and Linda Carli (2007) term the "leadership labyrinth." Followers may create a range of obstacles, or a "labyrinth," that hampers women leaders' effectiveness. These obstacles can include exclusion from networking opportunities, belittlement of women's communication styles and care work, and quotidian forms of disrespect, such as assigning women infantilizing nicknames (Diehl and Dzubinski 2017). Followers may contribute to structuring teams that lack representation of women or minorities, leading to tokenism. Even if follower actions are covert, such as sexual harassment, they may provoke public consequences for the leaders; for example, followers may ask more senior leaders to reorganize teams so that they do not have to work with women leaders (Diehl and Dzubinski 2017). Followers create discriminatory resistance implicitly or purposefully to interfere with women exercising leadership.

The racial dynamics of follower and leader relationships also guide whether and how participants create the double bind and the leadership labyrinth. White privilege has allowed followers and the media to prioritize white men and women's voices and experiences in social movements, resulting in the marginalization of women of color leaders (Hurwitz 2017; Reger 2015; B. Roth 2004). Furthermore, women of distinct racial/ethnic backgrounds endure particular stereotypes about their status as women, which condition their experiences of the double bind and barriers to leadership (Rosette et al. 2016). For example, sexualized stereotypes about black femininity as agentic as compared to Asian femininity may guide followers to penalize Asian women leaders if they act aggressively or penalize black women leaders if they are seen as being too soft (Le Espiritu 2008; Rosette et al. 2016). In general, followers who act on racist stereotypes intensify the harassment and hostility that women of color endure and mitigate penalties against white women.

Using rich ethnographic details about the leadership and followership dynamics in the Occupy movement, I provide a feminist and intersectional analysis of leadership stratification. Within the movement, many followers opposed the leadership of women and genderqueer persons of various races and ethnicities by acting on the double bind. Furthermore, followers created a leadership labyrinth that impeded women from becoming leaders or from executing leadership tasks. Followers created a labyrinth by harassing feminine leaders, practicing male dominance, and creating a hostile culture.

The Double Bind

Subtly or confrontationally, when followers object to women and genderqueer persons' agency and/or femininity, they create discriminatory resistance. Followers penalize women leaders for acting too boldly or not boldly enough. Occupy movement newspapers, zines, and interviewees reported many incidents where men rebelled against women's agency and sought to redirect meetings or protests. Lola, a black woman in Oakland, shares one experience:

> One young man in particular was talking over an older woman. He kept taking on the role of the facilitator, even though that was her role. There were other people saying, "Let her speak," and he didn't care. . . . Another young woman in her twenties had some sort of mental illness and was yelling next to our meeting. These three men got up, ran over to her, and started yelling at her. . . . [T]hey picked her up and physically carried

her out. I didn't know how to handle it at the time, it was so shocking. . . . I got up and left.

In this case, discriminatory resistance took the form of men physically and verbally competing with the woman who was attempting to lead the meeting. The followers also intimidated other people participating in the meeting, even manhandling the mentally ill woman, which demonstrated their physical masculine power over a weaker feminine woman. While the woman facilitator persisted, some followers sanctioned the men, and Lola left the meeting rather than confront them. When followers object to women's directions by interrupting, shouting, and physically controlling them, they endorse an informal gendered leadership hierarchy.

Lola experienced followers resisting women leaders according to a traditional gendered hierarchy of women's submissiveness and men's dominance. Physically and psychologically, followers modify how women lead. Sylvia Shaw's (2000) and Vicki Kramer, Alison Conrad, and Sumru Erkut's (2006) studies find that followers interrupt or debate even qualified women politicians and business leaders if they perceive them to be too weak *or* too bossy. Furthermore, Laurie Rudman and Kimberly Fairchild (2004) find that by threatening retaliation or sanctioning leaders, followers compel them to conform to gender stereotypes. Similarly, Katharina Pick (2017) argues that followers' resistance pressures women to act less powerful than men to avoid actual or potential threats of censorship and interruption. Guided by stereotypes about leadership, followers can profoundly reshape leadership dynamics.

Even during events spearheaded by women and feminists, followers sometimes use discriminatory resistance to assert gendered expectations about women leaders as being either too weak or too aggressive and men leaders as being more appropriate. At the first Occupy National Gathering (NatGat) Feminist General Assembly (FemGA) in Philadelphia, men co-opted a panel discussion:

The FemGA committee invited three men [two white and one of color] to explain how they support feminism and lead a discussion with other participants about supporting feminism. Instead, the men each explained how they embraced

feminism and the limits of feminism. Then, a man spontaneously handed the microphone to Chris Hedges [a Pulitzer
Prize–winning journalist, clergyman, and NatGat featured
speaker who was not scheduled to speak at the FemGA], who
explained that he sympathized with feminist struggles, but
as a white man, he is privileged and cannot be a feminist. A
woman of color indicated that it was time for the next agenda
item, and a white woman took over. (field notes, July 1, 2012)

This episode included several rotating leader-follower relationships.
Feminist leaders recruited men of different races who supported
feminism to take on informal leadership positions, expecting them
to lead a discussion about feminism at the FemGA. However, the men
spoke longer than arranged, went off-topic, and recruited a white
male leader to speak against feminism. The men promoted men's
voices and stories, which undermined the women who had created
the original agenda. They expressed discomfort with feminism and
reasserted their masculinity. Tristan Bridges (2010, 21) suggests that
men assert masculinity as they participate in feminist events because
they are not comfortable with feminism, or, as he puts it, "Feminist
politics in men are sometimes understood as a gender—and often
sexual—transgression." In addition, the men speaking at the FemGA
fell back on traditional gendered stereotypes about who is an appropriate leader when they spontaneously promoted a white man into
a leadership role at the feminist event. In this case, discriminatory
resistance was a double bind, suggesting that feminine leadership was
unlikable *and* illegitimate (Ridgeway 2011).

The above example alludes to the salience of gendered stereotypes, but racial hierarchies also affect the double bind. A leader-
follower interaction during a People of Color Caucus (POC) meeting
in New York illustrates this point. In an article in *Occupy N+1* (second issue), Audre Lim recounts a meeting where three black men
shouted over an Asian American woman facilitator and derailed the
agenda, whereupon Lim left, reflecting, "How I pitied [the facilita-
tor] as the cacophony grew." This episode is similar to the previous
example: followers took stock of a woman leader as she worked to
lead the meeting; they resisted the woman's agenda by shouting over
her, thereby avoiding her leadership and imposing a new agenda. Yet

discriminatory resistance may have been a result of followers being guided by gender and racial stereotypes. Research reveals a complex history of Asian Americans being stereotyped as "other" along a "black/white divide" and Asian Americans being discriminated against alongside black people as stereotypically "nonwhite" (Le Espiritu 2008, 124). Despite research that highlights historical coalitions between Asian American and black people in Third World activism (Le Espiritu 2008), followers at the POC may have critiqued the Asian American woman's leadership according to racial stereotypes about Asian Americans as "other" or inappropriate leaders as compared to black men. The *Occupy N+1* article characterizes the discriminatory resistance against the woman leader as unfounded, frustrating, and an example of gender discrimination, and it suggests that one of the men may have been an anti-Occupy "instigator" rather than a movement participant. The episode suggests that racial differences compound discriminatory resistance toward woman leaders.

Many Occupy participants advocated for women to run meetings and lead protests, yet women of various racial and ethnic backgrounds endured interruptions, shouting, and physical intimidation as they attempted to do so. In the examples analyzed here, discriminatory resistance took on the pattern of the double bind, and followers rejected women's leadership by supporting men's agency and critiquing and impeding agentic women.

The Leadership Labyrinth[2]

In addition to acting on gendered stereotypes, Occupy followers forced women and genderqueer persons to navigate a "leadership labyrinth," which limited their leadership (Eagly and Carli 2007). The following sections detail the barriers that impeded women and genderqueer leaders, including harassment, male dominance, and a hostile culture.

Harassment

Participants framed the Occupy movement as open and welcoming to the 99%, but followers' harassment limited how women and gender minorities accomplished leadership tasks. Discriminatory resistance in the form of harassment refers to catcalling and propositioning women for dates and sex. Sexual harassment becomes a barrier, because women and genderqueer persons are forced to dedicate energy to mitigating this behavior, thus supplanting the time and effort required for leadership responsibilities. Women leaders who endure sexual harassment suffer consequences that limit their advancement, including mental-health trauma, fear, depression, limited opportunities for collaboration, and even job loss (for a review, see Welsh 1999). Furthermore, when followers sexually harass women, they undermine effective communication between leaders and followers, thereby limiting women leaders' ability to perform at their jobs, let alone excel at them (Jackman 2006; Welsh 1999).

Common on city sidewalks and in parks where Occupy participants set up protest encampments, sexual harassment became an everyday obstacle for women who tried to take on leadership responsibilities. Participants reported about a dozen cases of sexual harassment and violence in the New York City encampment, several cases in Oakland, and more episodes in smaller cities (see, for example, Eschle 2016; Hardikar 2011; Lomax 2011; Newcomb 2011). Yet interviews, participant observation, and movement documents suggest that harassment was more of an everyday occurrence. For example, minutes from the November 6, 2011, Women Occupying Wall Street (WOWS) meeting in New York describe quotidian forms of harassment: "Three members shared personal experiences. . . . [One] entailed a man physically grabbing her arm while he had alcohol on his breath and declaring that she was sexy while several Occupiers looked on and laughed. We were unanimously disgusted by such incidents." Everyday forms of sexual harassment allowed followers to prioritize men's protest participation while marginalizing and undermining women's ability to protest or lead others. Similar to the example just cited, Luisa, a Latina woman from the Bay Area, describes feeling offended by a disrespectful follower: "This one guy hit on me, and I was like, 'Look, this is an organizing space,' and he's all like, 'Oh, you must be a feminist.'" The man who hit on Luisa not only sexually harassed her but undercut her authority and intimated that feminists are overly authoritative.

Followers may create physical, mental, and emotional hurdles for leaders to overcome in order to lead. Artemis, a young woman of mixed-race background from Oakland,[3] illustrates the difficulties of leading a general-assembly meeting: "There was no security, so anyone who wanted to could run up to the stage and get up in my face. Visibly intoxicated men were leering at me, and I was like, 'This is a hot mess!' It was overwhelming." Artemis played a visible, valuable, and powerful role by leading a large meeting, but belligerent male followers interacted with her as if she were a sex object. They did not follow her directions and ogled her to undermine her confidence and legitimacy. Also, Artemis reported that security at the event was lacking and contributed to an opportunity for harassment. She lamented the "hot mess," or the unbridled followers who attacked her. As a young woman of color, Artemis may have violated followers' gendered, racial, and age prejudices for who should lead. The belligerent men hampered Artemis's leadership by sexualizing and intimidating her. Later in the interview, Artemis reveals that she shifted her activism away from the main movement's organizations and toward the groups formed by feminists and people of color to evade harassment.

Followers utilized face-to-face and online harassment to deter women from leading. Sparrow, a white woman from the southern United States, describes how harassment affected her ability to play a major role in protests: "This troll guy would Tweet really disgusting things, like 'We are playing with our own feces' or 'Come and meet us for blow jobs.' . . . He had these accounts that made him sound in control, like @occupy__ and @thegeneralassembly__. I had symptoms of somebody being cyberstalked." Sparrow limited her participation because of the troll's harassment, which she likened to being followed threateningly online. Later in the interview, she reveals that she started using a masculine pseudonym online to hide her female identity and prevent the troll from harassing her even more. Sexual harassment constrained the extent to which women took on additional responsibilities and engaged in tasks with followers, tasks critical to becoming leaders. Similar to women whom followers sexually objectified and harassed in the New Left movement (Evans 1979), women in the Occupy movement found their authority limited by sexual harassment and violence. In both movements, women endured disrespect and were viewed as sex objects rather than as full-fledged activist leaders. Although feminist activists monitored emails, email discussion lists, Twitter accounts, and Facebook pages to try to limit harassers' actions, followers were still able to register their opposition to leaders by contacting them individually or harassing women's and feminist groups. Due to fear, intimidation, and critiques, women and genderqueer activists found that harassment became a barrier to leadership.

Followers who sexually harass leaders motivate them to find alternative outlets for leadership in groups in which they will not be harassed. A 2012 issue of the feminist zine *Quarrel* highlights women's and queer persons' fear of harassment and how Occupy participants created segregated spaces in response: "Almost every major city established women and or queer safe spaces, some that had people stand guard in shifts, as part of their strategies to create safety and respond to harassment and abuse." Taking on leadership roles in segregated feminist spaces with oppositional collective identities was a way for women and genderqueer persons to continue to participate in the overnight Occupy protests. However, these spaces also separated women and genderqueer people from the main movement's committees, limiting with whom they could accomplish leadership tasks and circumscribing the movement's inclusivity and diversity.

Male Dominance

Stereotypes about followers as passive or receptive are common. Yet followers can transform whole events. Discriminatory resistance in the form of male dominance refers to male followers changing a movement's strategy or tactics according to their actions. When male followers restructured strategies or tactics with the support of other men, they disrupted previously established strategies and tactics. For example, Dora, a white woman from Oakland, describes observing groups of male followers reorienting the intent of marches and events: "I don't know if it was the nature of being outside in the streets or what, but there were a lot of alpha males, and by default they took charge. Like when people were going to march against financial crimes, and it turned into this violent confrontation with police." Unclear about the racial composition of these groups of men, Dora describes mostly male followers who modified the movement's strategy without considering other leaders or safety issues. The men who took "charge" performed masculinity that valued men's voices and bodies, such as anger, aggressiveness, and decisiveness (Connell 2005).

In one example of male-dominated discriminatory resistance, a symbolic display protest disrupted the direction of a scheduled march:

> Eight men [two white and six of color from a range of ethnicities] covertly pitched a tent, a performance of occupation. The men sat in a circle around the tent and locked their arms in each other's, protecting the tent, demonstrating their strength. The action provoked a dozen police to violently crush the tent and arrest the men, while fifteen women and men attempted to de-escalate the police-protester clash by singing and humming in a separate circle. (field notes, June 30, 2012)

Although men *and* women leaders directed protesters to be nonviolent and not camp in a government park, this group of men followers symbolically "occupied" the park. The men created discriminatory resistance by forming a circle and provoking a clash with a majority-male police force. In opposition to such cooperative tactics as sitting in humming circles and nonviolently holding spaces, the men followers drew on practices of male dominance and male solidarity to disrupt the ongoing protest and shift it into a new direction, which resulted in the police breaking up the entire group. These followers created hurdles for the established leaders, who had planned a peaceful and nonconfrontational march in city-designated "free-speech" areas. Instead of continuing the march, leaders had to shift their focus toward calming activities to stop the police sweep. Followers who spark high-risk physical confrontations with a mostly male police force excel in what Deborah Tannen (1995, 144) terms "ritual opposition," or verbal confrontations, fighting, intimidation, and physical displays of strength, which prioritizes masculine leadership. When groups of men orchestrate high-risk protest strategies, male-dominated ritual opposition creates a barrier to other leaders' plans.

In Occupy encampments and meetings, participants used large group discussions to strategize protest actions, and anyone present could enter the debates. Participants communicated to large groups without electronic sound-amplification systems by using "mic checks," a call-and-response ritual wherein speakers shouted and crowds repeated the speakers' words. During mic checks, the person leading had to speak up and project. At the same time, the followers surrounding the speaker had to listen closely enough to repeat the leader's words. It was common for spontaneous mic checks to devolve into shouting matches, such as in this episode at NatGat in Philadelphia:

> A woman did a mic check, and a man with a bullhorn interrupted her and started a mic check more loudly as he stared down over her (the man of color was about 5'8" [and] 160 pounds, and the white woman was about 5'2" and 110 pounds). Another man tried to interrupt the man, but the first said, "I am not done talking yet." No one interrupted [either of] these men (who appeared to be men of color of different races). (field notes, June 30, 2012)

Representative of the more spontaneous protests that Occupy participants used to lead followers, this mic check benefitted the louder, larger man instead of the quieter, smaller woman. While the man prevented other men from interrupting, the woman did not. The group of men spoke more frequently and loudly, creating a barrier to the woman's leadership. However, the followers also empowered marginalized men of color to speak. Although she does not detail follower reactions, Kathleen Blee (2012) finds that grassroots groups shift conversations toward the suggestions of men over women and toward white people over people of color. She also finds that groups ignore women's and people of color's suggestions. During this particular mic check, discriminatory resistance as male dominance penalized the woman but also mitigated white privilege.

Male dominance was a constant concern for Occupy participants. Some groups opposed male dominance proactively. For example, a primarily white street theater group from New York dramatized the baseball team of the 1%, the "Tax Dodgers." The group also included a Hula-Hooping cheerleading squad, the "Corporate Loopholes." They orchestrated rousing sing-alongs and street theater performances during encampments. The male "Tax Dodgers" wore beards, strutted, and flexed their muscles. The women "Corporate Loopholes" wore traditional cheerleading outfits with red miniskirts, styled their long hair in ponytails, and playfully bounced and jumped to exude femininity. Despite performing activist street theater within the nonhierarchical Occupy movement, the men played more central leadership roles as the macho baseball players. According to interviews with participants, many of the women activists were uncomfortable portraying cheerleaders, feeling uneasy and marginalized when asked to perform hyperfemininity. In response, the group debated whether to let women cross-dress and join the men on the baseball team, allowing them to share more central roles. On the other side of the debate, some were concerned that cross-dressing would detract from the objective of the street theater: to portray the 1% as excessively gender normative. In the end, a few women acted as the macho ball players, although no men cross-dressed as "Loopholes." In this case, followers provided feedback to each other and the male director of the group to adjust the casting, and the group modified a leadership barrier that had excluded women from the more central roles. Participants' racial homogeneity as a nearly all-white group likely contributed to the ease with which they made the adjustment.

Conscious about leadership stratification, Occupy participants frequently encouraged women and genderqueer persons of all racial/ethnic backgrounds and men of color to take on leadership responsibilities. The movement ethos for sharing leadership was termed "step-up and step-back" (Maharawal 2016). Molly, a mixed-race woman from the western United States,[4] explains:

> If you are a white man and you have spoken already, you have to wait. You have to wait for other people to talk. And if you are an indigenous person who is used to being quiet and marginalized, you have to find your power, claim it, and step up and speak, so there is a shared power. That is what we are going for.

As one of the bottom-liners of her Occupy group, Molly supported the step-up and step-back tactic to limit male dominance and racism among followers and the movement's informal and rotating leaders. Some feminist activists recognized recurrent male dominance and required the implementation of step-up and step-back tactics. Lorriana, a white woman bottom-liner in New York, explains:

> We would get press releases with draft quotes, and if it was
> all men, or white men, we would be like, "Hi—what are the
> women organizing?" We tried for gender parity here, [because
> Occupy was] really talking about changing up the conversa-
> tion. But if you just had a bunch of talking white men repre-
> senting us, then what did it matter?

In scenarios where men did not include women's voices on press
releases, Lorriana recognized women's absence. By questioning the
people who submitted the press releases, she opposed male dominance that silenced women's views in the media.

Like step-up and step-back, Occupy facilitators sometimes reor-
dered lists of speakers to allow women and racial minorities to speak
before white men, a process the movement termed "progressive stack."
Progressive stack limited male dominance during meetings and events
by requiring white men to speak less and after women of various races
and men of color. Step-up and step-back and progressive stack were
attempts to disrupt followers' affinity for white male dominance. Although many groups employed step-up and step-back and progressive
stack methods, the procedures were not required. When such practices
to mitigate discriminatory resistance were not enforced, followers often
chose to fall back on traditional gender and racial status hierarchies.

A Hostile Culture

An organizational culture encompasses the aesthetics, beliefs, com-
munications, rituals, and values shared among people within a particular context. A group of followers can produce an organizational
culture that provides opportunities for or limits the development of
particular leaders. Followers create hostile cultures by acting on and
reinforcing gender and racial stereotypes. Hostile organizational
cultures prioritize white men who perform aggression, competition,
and confrontation. Therefore, participants in hostile cultures limit
whether and how women, genderqueer persons, and men of color
lead. Within a hostile culture, not only are harassment and male dominance commonplace; a range of other interactions create a "chilly"
environment where especially women and genderqueer persons from
a range of races and ethnicities feel isolated and unimportant. Women

and genderqueer persons of color in sexist environments weather the intersection of racial prejudice and sexism and increased unfriendliness as compared to white participants. Crystal Hoyt and Susan Murphy (2016) reveal that majority-male groups, masculine-coded environments, masculine cultural symbols, sexist men, or even just the knowledge that sexism and sexist men are part of an organization harm women's ability to lead and be respected as leaders. Moreover, Susan Sturm (2001) argues that loose and decentralized organizations are more likely to foster hidden sexism. Sexism and racism may motivate women and genderqueer persons, especially people of color, to choose to exclude themselves from leadership to avoid hostility. Even cultural contexts that appear to be gender neutral or diverse may harbor sexism or racism and limit who can lead within them. Hostile cultures are a form of discriminatory resistance that limits leadership by women, especially women of color, who experience the intersection of gender and racial inequalities.

Art, music, theater, and cultural practices in the Occupy movement that replicated hypermasculine cultures contributed to the unintelligibility of women and genderqueer persons' leadership. For example, the inside back cover of the March 2012 issue of *Tidal*, a movement newspaper, amplifies masculine cultures exclusive of women: the full-page image depicts a matador atop a police car, waving a red flag at *Charging Bull*. By symbolizing bullfighting, a male-dominated sport devoted to torturing and killing a ferocious male animal, the image conveys the Occupy movement as fighting Wall Street and the police and valuing masculine competition. As an example of the aesthetics and rituals of the Occupy movement, the image represents a hostile organizational culture that prioritized white men leaders and violence.

Followers may reinforce stereotypes about women's and genderqueer persons' marginal positions in an organization by replicating explicitly masculine cultures, art, music, or cultural practices that often exclude women. For example, during high-profile events, the New York–based Guitarmy Occupy spin-off group followed Tom Morello from the band Rage Against the Machine. In the group of musicians who strummed guitars and sang protest songs, men gravitated to center stage and sometimes played bare-chested to call attention to their masculine bodies, while token women performers stayed in the background. Guitarmy followers drew on and replicated the male-dominated culture of the rock-music industry, reproducing a culture that marginalizes women musicians and limits women and gender-queer leadership (Schippers 2002).

Although many participants reported that Occupy encampments became a temporary society where people shared free food and easily developed friendships, volunteers formed security teams to monitor some participants who stole from others or were overly intoxicated. Security teams supervised aggressive antagonistic participants to protect more vulnerable participants. To respond to fear and aggression generated by sexism and racism, feminist and queer participants in the Safer Spaces group in New York City created a "Community Agreement," a pledge for movement participants to vow to "subvert the histories and structures of oppression that marginalize and divide us." Still, many Occupy participants felt unwelcome, unimportant, isolated, or excluded. In the feminist zine *Quarrel*, a transgender person of color explains:

> There hadn't really been an established area where I felt comfortable. . . . A lot of people were angry and seemed to have a very militant attitude when giving instructions. . . . I felt pushed to the side. It felt very heavily dominated with a "White Male Privilege Hetero" climate.

This person believed that the encampment was a combative and uncomfortable environment due to sexism, racism, and the marginalization of queer people. Feeling unwelcome, this individual and other genderqueer persons and persons of color believed that they could not engage in activism, let alone leadership.

Hostile environments create conditions that normalize patterns of submissiveness and dominance. The first issue of the feminist zine *Workin' on It! We Activate! We Agitate! Womyn of Color Occupy Wall Street & Beyond* documents everyday resentment directed toward women of color and transgender participants in the movement:

> Many of us experienced or witnessed slurs, attacks. . . . When we attempted to challenge these abuses, we were silenced or ostracized. . . . [W]e have identified a shadow leadership

structure. . . . The result is heightened anxiety and/or suspi-
cion of women of color and/or queer voices who challenge organizing practices.

When followers stifle women's and genderqueer persons' decisions
and use confrontational nicknames to undermine their actions, they
create obstacles, or, as *Working on It!* Terms it, an exclusive "shadow
leadership structure." These forms of discriminatory resistance were
similar to those used by some allies and spin-offs of Black Lives Matter, groups that ultimately exploited the work done by queer black
women leaders. Alicia Garza (2014), one of the queer black women
founders of the Black Lives Matter movement, argues that a range of
potential followers "erased" the leadership of queer black women and
produced "hetero-patriarchal" inequalities and racism when they co-
opted the "Lives Matter" slogan and created spin-off groups opposed
to the mission of the Black Lives Matter movement:

> We completely expect those who benefit directly and improp-
> erly from White supremacy to try and erase our existence. We
> fight that every day. But when it happens amongst our allies, we
> are baffled, we are saddened, and we are enraged. And it's time
> to have the political conversation about why that's not okay.

When followers deny women and queer people of color responsibility
or credibility, illegitimacy inhibits these potential leaders' own psychological state, their ability to assert authority, and their desire to accomplish extra work (Rosette et al. 2016). As Andrea Vial, Jaime Napier,
and Victoria Brescoll (2016, 410) suggest, constant antagonism toward
women leaders may create a "troublesome self-reinforcing cycle of
illegitimacy." By creating discriminatory resistance in the form of a
hostile environment, Occupy followers reinforced the racialized gendered prejudice that white men were the only legitimate leaders.

Conclusion

The third issue of *N+1 Occupy! An OWS-Inspired Gazette* includes
an article titled "Some Issues with Horizontalism," in which scholar-
activist Marina Sitrin argues that how activists listen to each other

influences who leads and who follows: "Depending on the circumstances I think there are many ways we listen differently and sometimes more actively to one person over another. I see this differential listening as related to the question of leadership. If one person's voice is heard more, are they not a leader in some way?" Although rarely discussed or studied, inequalities within nonhierarchical social movements preclude inclusivity and intersectionality.

I have explored these overarching research questions: Under what conditions do movement cultures exclude or alienate particular individuals and groups—especially for movement leadership? How do gender and race processes influence contemporary social movement dynamics and culture?

I argue that traditional cultural beliefs about gender and race influenced who led the Occupy movement and how they did so. If followers are guided by stereotypical beliefs about men being ideal leaders, they devalue, exclude, and alienate women and genderqueer leaders. Likewise, followers' stereotypical beliefs about white persons as ideal leaders marginalize leaders of color. At the intersection of gender and racial stereotypes, followers diminish women of color's and genderqueer people of color's leadership. These dynamics limit diverse leadership, inclusivity, and intersectional praxis within contemporary social movements.

Examples in this chapter demonstrate how discriminatory resistance in the Occupy movement was similar to intersectional conflicts about leadership in workplaces and institutionalized politics. Studies of hierarchical organizations reveal that followers are more often uncooperative and even destructive toward women and genderqueer leaders of all races and ethnicities as compared to white men (Rudman and Fairchild 2004; Rudman and Mescher 2013). Followers who are guided by gendered and racial prejudices fall back on and recreate traditional gender and racial hierarchies.

Despite the ideal that leaderlessness sparks greater participation, the loose leadership structure of the Occupy movement gave followers the leeway to create a gendered and racial stratification of leadership even within the "nonhierarchical" setting. In interactional and informal leader-follower relationships, when followers refuse to act on women's and queer persons' leadership, they reward men's leadership. The discriminatory resistance that characterized the Occupy movement demonstrates that its leadership practices were based on neither intersectional inclusivity nor the belief that anyone could be a leader. Instead, discriminatory resistance facilitated leadership among people who entered this social movement with greater privilege and power. Most leaders in a social movement are men of its dominant racial identity, such as black men leading civil rights movements or white men leading environmental movements (Morris and Staggenborg 2004). Here, I have shown how discriminatory resistance was a mechanism for the continuing marginalization of women, queer, and racial minority leaders in the Occupy movement. How leaders and followers respond to each other according to gender, race, class, and other status hierarchies ultimately determines whether a movement will embody the intersectional imperative or become exclusive to white male leaders.

4

Women Occupying Wall Street

Mobilizing Feminism within Occupy

F eminists involved in Occupy and other not-explicitly feminist
social movements that emerged in the 2000s and 2010s[1] created
LIES: A Journal of Materialist Feminism.[2] Using a crowd-funded
Kickstarter[3] campaign, they financed a physical publication and an
online version of the journal. The articles expose the "gendered fault
lines" (LIES Collective 2012, 9) within contemporary activism. An
article in the first volume, titled "On the Recent #Occupations: Com-
munique from W.&.T.C.H., Halloween 2011, Baltimore, Amerikkka,"
critiques the absence of feminist analysis and intersectional praxis
within the Occupy movement:

> What other percentages hide behind the nearly-whole 99%? . . .
> The quarter of women that will get sexually assaulted in their
> lifetime? . . . Is a woman of color's experience of the crisis in-
> terchangeable with that of the white man whose wage is twice
> hers? . . . For now, we are simply critiquing this occupation for

An earlier version of Chapter 4 was previously published as Hurwitz, Heather
McKee and Verta Taylor, "Women Occupying Wall Street: Gender Conflict and
Feminist Mobilization." From *100 Years of the Nineteenth Amendment: An Ap-
praisal of Women's Political Activism*, edited by Lee Ann Banasak and Holly J.
McCammon. © 2018 Oxford University Press. Reproduced with permission of the
Licensor through PLSclear.

assuming we are there, while we have so far been left out. . . .
[W]e radical feminist, anti-racist revolutionaries are going to
keep bringing our bodies and ideologies to the occupation.

W.&.T.C.H, the collective of authors behind the article, evaluates the
idea of the 99% from an intersectional feminist perspective. The writers argue that the Occupy movement glossed over women's experiences
of gender inequality, such as sexual assault and the wage gap, that are
critical to understanding women's experiences of financial inequality.
Throughout the article, they argue that the 99% identity obscures the
intersections of class, race, gender, and sexual inequalities. They critique white men's voices and experiences in the Occupy movement as
overly dominant and exclusive of the experiences of women, especially
women of color. Although participants in the Occupy movement practiced a range of different feminist politics, most feminists criticized the
movement for analyzing class inequality incorrectly by not considering
the intersections of economic, race, and gender inequality.

Feminists contributed in a variety of ways to the Occupy mobilizations. The W.&.T.C.H article is an exemplary record of contemporary feminist media activism that challenged *and* contributed to
the Occupy movement. Although its authors criticize participants
in Occupy for excluding "radical feminist, anti-racist revolutionaries," the article provides evidence of feminists engaging in substan-
tial dialogue within the movement. W.&.T.C.H members assert that
feminism will continue to influence contemporary activism when
they vow to "keep bringing our bodies and ideologies to the occupation." These writers participated in the momentum of Occupy and
created intersectional and feminist media about it and about feminism. They represent many feminists who created media, provided
resources, garnered support, and amalgamated feminist activism
during the momentum of the Occupy protests.

Feminist organizing within the Occupy movement often embodied
the intersectional imperative and critiqued activism bereft of intersectional praxis. I draw on a rich and extensive ethnography of feminist activism within the movement to illustrate three research questions: How
did Occupy participants build solidarity across gender, race, class, and
sexual identities within the mass movement? Under what conditions
do movement cultures exclude or alienate particular individuals and
groups? How do gender, race, class, and sexuality processes influence

contemporary social movement dynamics and culture? Women and genderqueer persons brought feminism into many different spaces within the Occupy movement via three processes. Sparked by the shock and injustice of gender conflict,[4] participants developed feminist collective identities, feminist "free spaces," and feminist bridge leaders from within the movement. Acting more quickly and decisively than feminists who addressed chauvinism within mass movements in the 1970s (Evans 1979; B. Roth 2004), feminist Occupiers used these three processes to spread feminist politics, ideals, and protests from nearly the beginning of the movement. They addressed inequalities in their everyday movement work by using intersectionality as a "critical mode of inquiry" and action: they revealed unequal power relations based on gender, race, and sexual hierarchies and then acted to transform them (P. Collins and Bilge 2016). They brought a variety of feminist politics to bear on Occupy dynamics that otherwise did not achieve intersectional praxis. They became a key force in motivating the intersectional imperative within the movement.

Feminist Organizations and Occupy

Feminists contributed to nearly every major action in the Occupy movement, starting with the initial planning and first days of the first encampment in New York City. Women and feminists in particular raised complaints about sexism and white male dominance in movement committees, organizations, newspapers, and general assemblies. Some of the early sources of gender conflict were women's and queer participants' grievances about sexual harassment, belligerent men, and a lack of democracy within the encampments. They debated whether they could sleep safely at the urban protest encampments. They questioned whether they were welcome to participate when loud white men dominated the leadership positions. Feminists revealed that although leaders in the main Occupy movement espoused the goal of inclusivity, at the same time, gender, sexual, and racial inequalities limited the extent to which the encampments became welcoming and safe spaces for everyone. Gender conflicts motivated infighting, and yet they also sparked feminist mobilization and the formation of explicitly feminist organizations, media, cultural practices, and meetings.

Feminist activism within the Occupy movement facilitated the inclusion of women's and genderqueer participants' grievances. In spaces led by feminist leaders and informed by a feminist oppositional collective identity, participants challenged gender inequality in the movement's daily activities, goals, and tactics (Brunner 2011; M. Butler 2011; Maharawal 2011). Benefiting from 1960s' and 1970s' feminist activists, contemporary feminist participants, and millennial college students, Occupiers developed a variety of feminist organizations and networks to mobilize women's participation in the movement. In addition to creating explicitly feminist organizations, they participated in the main movement's organizations and working groups, such as sanitation and sustainability committees. They responded to gender conflict in the main movement's organizations and the feminist subgroups with the goal of strengthening the Occupy movement. Contention around women's subordination across the main movement created an opportunity for feminist organizations to use Occupy's momentum to channel the activism of existing feminists toward it and to recruit new individuals to feminism.

Experienced feminist activists recognized and responded to gender conflict. Feminists were able to organize within the Occupy movement due to its open, porous, voluntary, and "leaderless" structure. In addition, the large number of encampments and protest events provided opportunities for feminists to contribute to mass actions. Frustrated by the male-dominated leadership and culture of the Occupy movement and the sexual harassment in the encampments, feminists, women, sexual minorities, and genderqueer and transgender participants first turned to existing feminist organizations and networks to mobilize. Over time, however, feminist participants increasingly began to create separate feminist organizations within the Occupy movement. A variety of feminist organizations with goals of increasing the feminist presence in Occupy and mobilizing larger numbers of participants overall emerged within the first year.

Preexisting Feminist Organizations That Joined Occupy

A variety of feminist organizations, collectives, and institutions activated feminists within the Occupy movement. National and local feminist reading circles, self-defense collectives, nongovernmental organizations (NGOs), lesbian and gay groups, and other feminist networks in New York City and the San Francisco Bay Area recruited feminists to Occupy. Influential feminists, including Judith Butler, Angela Davis, Eve Ensler, Jo Freeman, Ursula K. Le Guin, Gloria Steinem, Alice Walker, and many more, blogged, wrote articles, and visited and spoke at occupations to support the movement. Bloggers and journalists for *Ms.* magazine and *The Feminist Wire*, among other feminist publications, promoted Occupy and delivered critical commentary about the movement. Women's studies programs and women's cultural, musical, and artistic communities also provided resources to local Occupy movements.

Several national feminist organizations shared resources and personnel as they participated in Occupy mobilizations. For example, CODEPINK and the Feminist Peace Network (FPN) sponsored http://www.womenoccupy.org and http://occupypatriarchy.org, respectively. The websites served as communication hubs and provided tools for feminist organizing. CODEPINK personnel participated in planning the September 17, 2011, emergence of Occupy Wall Street (OWS) and continued to mobilize with Occupy throughout the first year of the movement. CODEPINK members responded to the lack of women's opportunities to speak to the press by organizing speak-outs against gender inequality and contributed articles to *Ms.* magazine. They published media guides on http://www.womenoccupy.org to train women to speak to the press about their experiences. Also, they sponsored face-to-face media trainings. CODEPINK members taught activists how to use Twitter and other social media with "live Tweeting" workshops. Their sponsored website, http://www.womenoccupy.org, became a clearinghouse of feminist organizations. The site listed local women's groups and publicized the feminist actions they deployed to support the Occupy movement. In addition, CODEPINK activists contributed to the September 2012 Occupy "birthday" protest in New York City. They distributed flyers with the slogan "Bust Up Bank of America!" The flyers also included times and locations to protest with CODEPINK, sign-up information to receive text alerts about protests by CODEPINK and other Occupy organizers, numbers to call to receive jail support from the National Lawyers Guild, and a list of women's demands for Bank of America, such as, "Break up into smaller, safer banks! Stop funding dirty coal. Pay the statutorily required 35% corporate income tax." Although its base in New York City allowed the organization to play a particularly active role in the New York Occupy movement, CODEPINK sponsored Occupy-related actions throughout the country by mobilizing its preexisting activist network.

Using a range of tactics under the umbrella of media activism, participants in the FPN, especially Lucinda Marshall, exposed sexism and misogyny within the Occupy movement on the blog http://occupypatriarchy.org. For example, a post published on January 19, 2012, advocates for readers to complete an online petition against sexual assault at Occupy Boston. A January 31, 2012, entry reposted from the Occupy Dixie blog exposes gender conflict at Occupy Nashville. Other blog posts reveal how men excluded women from speaking at meetings and from speaking with the press. On December 6, 2011, the FPN also launched an online radio show. The inaugural episode features Robin Morgan, a feminist icon, scholar, founder of the Sisterhood Is Global Institute, and cofounder of the Women's Media Center. On the show, she analyzes the relationship between feminism and the Occupy movement and argues, "[Occupy] will fail without women and feminists."

In the streets and online, experienced feminists mobilized communities of feminist peace activists to support the Occupy movement and to support new feminist activism. They garnered support from national feminist networks to contribute to the Occupy movement. They blogged and reposted entries from other feminist blogs. In short, feminists contributed a range of innovative street and online tactics as a part of the Occupy mobilizations.

New Feminist Spin-Off Organizations

Occupy participants also created feminist organizations unique to the movement. Within the first two weeks of the movement's emergence, women and feminists found themselves confronted by male dominance, and the ensuing gender conflict led women to establish separate organizational spaces. An article in the first issue of *Occupy! N+1* highlights the problem of male dominance and a growing concern regarding gender inequality in the movement: "I've never felt as marginalized and unsafe as the first night I arrived at OWS. . . . There were men everywhere. I would estimate men outnumbered women sleeping in the park three to one" (E. Smith 2011, 9). Ellie Smith and other women Occupiers formed a Women's Caucus within the first two weeks of the New York City encampment's establishment to create a safer, designated space for women to sleep so they would not wake up next to strange men.

Although some feminists addressed class, gender, racial, and sexual inequalities, some focused more centrally on "women." At OWS, a variety of groups emerged that were inspired by a range of different kinds of feminist politics, including the Speakeasy Caucus, Women Occupying Wall Street (WOWS), the Feminist General Assembly (FemGA), Women Occupying Nations, Divine Feminine, the Queer Caucus, Anti-racism Allies, Strong Women Rules, the People of Color Caucus (POC), and the Queer/LGBTIQA2Z Caucus.[5] For example, minutes from the New York City General Assembly posted on its website indicated that on October 17, 2011, feminists publicized that the Speakeasy Caucus was "open to both male-bodied and female-bodied individuals for the purpose of discussion, for how to make this community a safe space for everyone to have their voices heard truly equally." The group became a watchdog, calling out sexism in the media and the movement. Speakeasy Caucus members also had a significant influence on gender parity in interviews fielded by OWS participants in New York City, as Kate explains:

> *The Colbert Report* had sent a reporter down, and I think they interviewed three guys and showed, but didn't interview, one topless woman. So we sent this letter on behalf of the Speakeasy Caucus that the coverage was sexist. The main author of the letter was a woman who went by the name "Ketchup." Then a few days later, *The Colbert Report* people sent us a press request for another interview. There was this whole debate within the Speakeasy press team of who to send—either Ketchup or a woman of color or someone else. And meanwhile, the other man who ended up being on the show, Justin, had independently agreed to go on the show, and so then *The Colbert Report* contacted us and said, "We've got it covered, thanks so much." We were like, "NO!" Those of us who knew that Ketchup had written the letter said it has to be her on the show. It almost didn't happen at all but ended up being a compromise.

Feminists exposed sexist practices among reporters and fought to place women and queer speakers in interviews. In this instance, they ensured that a man *and* a woman appeared on *The Colbert Report* television show on October 31, 2011. The feminist spin-off groups, such as the Speakeasy Caucus, worked with participants on the main OWS press team to recognize when women were denied interviews with the press and to motivate and train women and queer people to participate in interviews.

One of the most significant transformations among the spin-off groups inspired by feminist politics was when WOWS shifted its activities from serving primarily as a discussion group to taking responsibility for FemGAs. FemGAs became a new mobilizing structure for feminist activism, because they allowed for the mobilization of feminism within Occupy but simultaneously contributed to feminist movements. FemGAs served as free spaces for the recruitment of women, and gender and sexual minorities to Occupy, and feminist activism. At the same time, FemGAs mobilized support for the Occupy movement overall. Shirin, an active participant who often bottom-lined aspects of the FemGAs, explains:

> The purpose of the Women Occupying Wall Street group was evolving, and the FemGA concept really arose from the idea of turning into an outreach organization where people who were already working on feminist issues in New York could come and have an assembly. Basically, it was for Occupy, but we could connect to [feminists] who were already doing this work and get more people connected with Occupy in that way.

FemGAs flourished in the spring and summer of 2012, a time when most Occupy encampments had been dismantled. The FemGAs mirrored the Occupy movement's general-assemblies tactic. By building on the momentum of the Occupy movement, FemGAs also mobilized support for feminism.

In the San Francisco Bay Area, the main feminist spin-off organizations were the SF Women's Alliance and Oakland Occupy Patriarchy (OOP). The SF Women's Alliance created safe spaces within the San Francisco encampments. Members built solidarity and oppositional consciousness among participants by sharing their reasons for being a part of the occupation and their sexist, racist, and homophobic experiences at the encampments and in their lives in general. They spearheaded a rousing International Women's Day march in 2012 and rallied in front of the Federal Reserve and other banks. Marchers supported reproductive rights and protested sexual harassment and sexism in the banking industry. OOP members led key Occupy marches and actions in Oakland. For example, they led one of the contingents in the massive Oakland General Strike on November 2, 2011, that collectively stopped all truck traffic and effectively all commerce at the Port of Oakland, one of the largest in the United States. OOP members also played a central role in attempts by Occupy Oakland (OO) to reclaim and re-occupy their encampment in Frank Ogawa Plaza (also known as Oscar Grant Plaza) and other spaces in 2011 and 2012. They organized as a "feminist bloc" or a "glitter bloc," using such feminine-gendered tactics as donning glittery, pink, and/or purple clothing; wearing sequined face masks (instead of the black face masks typically worn by black bloc anarchists); and carrying banners with such slogans as "Disarm Cops, Arm Feminists" and "Feminists and Queers Against Capitalism." OOP was another example of a feminist group committed to organizing for feminism *and* Occupy, as evidenced by an excerpt from its points of unity posted online: "Women, Trans people, Queers, Fags, Dykes, need a space that is OURS. We are marginalized, harassed, and attacked in other spaces all the time. . . . [W]e think we can support each other and increase our power by working together."[6]

A few feminist spin-off groups embraced "queer feminism." Participants in OOP, several New York City feminist spin-off groups, and the Queer/LGBTIQA2Z Caucus in New York City most commonly referred to themselves as "queer feminists." These groups loosely referred to queer feminism as advocating for transgender rights and other issues related to queer sexuality as a part of the larger goals of feminism. In addition to drawing on feminist tactical repertoires, participants in these groups borrowed protest tactics from lesbian, gay, transgender, and queer movements. Participants in the groups brought together practices from second-wave feminists, feminist consciousness-raising circles, Gaga Feminism politics, the queer/transgender politics of contemporary feminists, and the transgender rights movement (Halberstam 2012; Reger 2012). Like lesbian feminists of the 1980s and 1990s (Taylor and Whittier 1992), feminists in these groups often wore typically masculine clothes, such as flannel shirts and Doc Marten boots; had asymmetrical haircuts; did not shave their armpits or legs; and adopted men's or androgynous nicknames, such as "Ken" or "Sam." Alex encapsulates how these groups merged queer and feminist politics:

> What brought me to the group was that they were putting the words "queer" and "feminist" together—and it had been years since anybody had tried to do that! For about the last fifteen years, it had been sort of like "feminism" had been a bad word. But now, I felt like we were trying to find a place where people could come and talk about women's issues, however they were perceived, and with the development of the trans movement, figure out how you could make a feminist and/or women's liberation movement without putting it in gender-binary terms. There was all this confusion and tension, and that was very much a part of our group. A good example of the tension was an anti-right-to-life march. One of my friends was trying to make a leaflet. She was trying to say abortion is a women's issue. I said, "No, you can't say that, because some people may not identify with being a woman and may need an abortion. Legal abortion is a women's issue most of the time, but now it is also an issue for genderqueer or trans persons as well."

Alex is representative of participants in the feminist spin-off groups in Occupy who frequently debated queer feminism. They mobilized around feminist politics and transgender rights. Queer feminist participants deployed such tactics as using Preferred Gender Pronouns (also known as PGPs or gender pronouns) and circulating a statement titled "OWS Must Resist Cis-Supremacy and Trans-Misogyny," an open letter that exposed transphobic hate speech and discrimination against trans persons in Occupy encampments. Feminist spin-off groups that embraced queer feminism advocated for transgender and genderqueer rights as a part of practicing feminism.

One key example of national feminist organizing that emerged from within the movement was the Occupy National Gathering (NatGat) FemGA, a collaborative effort between WOWS, FemGA groups, the Philadelphia-based NatGat planning committee, and groups linked to http://www.womenoccupy.org. Through Maestro online conference calls, participants across the nation discussed the purpose of the FemGA and its potential impact. Hundreds of diverse Occupiers participated in the NatGat FemGA on July 1, 2012. To put the national spotlight on Philadelphia with a feminist and Occupy presence, several activists who had participated in the FemGA decided to "Occupy the 4th of July" by interrupting the annual reading of the Declaration of Independence on Independence Mall. Activists stood in the front row in silent protest, wearing pink letters that spelled "Revolution Now." Many of the activists who met at the Nat-Gat FemGA reconvened as the FemForce affinity group for the Occupy birthday party on September 17, 2012. During several days of action that included anti-banking, anti-fracking, and pro-Occupy marches and encampments, it was not uncommon for women, queer people, or even straight men who participated with FemForce to use feminine-gendered tactics, such as chanting, "Bust up big banks" as they stopped along the march routes and flung bras at Bank of America branches.

A variety of feminist organizations and protests enlivened the Occupy movement. Feminist activists acted on the intersectional imperative by bringing together analyses of gender and class oppressions and forming coalitions with preexisting feminist movements. But what were the interactive processes behind the development of these organizations? What social forces created the opportunity for feminist protests and the influence of feminism within this not-explicitly feminist mass movement?

Three Processes Mobilizing Feminism

Feminists in the separate feminist organizations and those within the main Occupy organizations opposed gender conflict and mobilized for feminism. Although gender conflict harmed many women, transgender, and feminist activists, it also triggered feminists to develop a feminist collective identity, feminist "free spaces," and feminist bridge leaders. These three processes illustrate ways in which feminists can navigate and influence not-explicitly feminist social movements and work to implement intersectional praxis.

Feminist Collective Identity

Gender conflict sparked opportunities for feminists to forge feminist collective identities. By developing "feminist collective identities," activists erect a boundary between themselves and anti-feminist beliefs and practices. They create feminist collective identities to build solidarity among feminists within a social movement. Drawing on their shared beliefs about ending all forms of inequality, they support the empowerment of women, genderqueer persons, and racial and sexual minorities. Occupy participants developed feminist collective identities to oppose gendered, racial, and sexual inequalities that they endured within the movement's male-dominated culture. For example, incidents of gender and sexual harassment triggered feminist solidarity. Imogen explains how gender conflict inspired feminist organizing and forms of online consciousness raising:

> We got broadsided with reports of people saying, "I feel really intimidated, I was harassed, I was hit upon," whatever, all of these reports. And we put up the Facebook page really quickly, and people started migrating there and sharing stories. . . . I think that forged a number of opportunities for people to work together.

Imogen described how gender conflict motivated conversations among women and feminists within the movement that led to the participants raising each other's consciousness about gender inequality. She credited gender conflict as initiating oppositional consciousness, which led to the development of solidarity among feminists. Furthermore, participants posted their views on a Facebook page dedicated to airing gender conflicts and resisting male domination. Using this new (at the time) form of social media, participants amplified women's grievances and provided an initial online space where they could develop a collective identity in opposition to gender conflict.

Offline, in the encampments, feminist participants and survivors of sexual assault also mobilized feminist solidarity. On November 4, 2011, a group within the New York encampment calling themselves members of a sexual-assault survivor's team issued a statement on the New York General Assembly website:

We are creating and sharing strategies that educate and transform our community into a culture of consent, safety, and well-being. At OWS, these strategies currently include support circles, counseling, consent trainings, safer sleeping spaces, self-defense trainings, community watches, awareness campaigns and other evolving community-based processes to address harm.

Members of this group formed the Safer Spaces Working Group to develop feminist consciousness about sexual assault. Over the course of the following three months, they negotiated a "Community Agreement" to spread feminist consciousness more broadly in the movement. They increased awareness about gender conflict, male dominance, and homophobia. The Community Agreement was a kind of pledge for movement participants to, among other commitments, "support the empowerment of each person in order to subvert the histories and structures of oppression that marginalize and divide us, such as racism, sexism, classism, heterosexism, transphobia, religious discrimination, ageism, & ableism." Participants wearing pink "Safer Spaces" armbands became on-the-ground spokespersons pushing for recognition of the Community Agreement. In addition, they often served as confidants and advocates for other survivors, such as Ivy:

> I tried to be a mediator for this kind of thing. I was trying to be an advocate for speaking out in the park. I was really trying to reach out to these kids who had been sexually assaulted, but it was so hard to get them to go to the authorities. They didn't want to do a rape kit test, and they didn't want to deal with the police, so a lot of those instances, you know, were just left to speculation by the media. I knew all of the instances that happened to these kids. They would come to me, and they would tell me, but they wouldn't do anything about it, so I was forced to listen to them telling me these horrific scenarios, and there was no justice for them. I couldn't force them, you know.

Transient youth who experienced sexual assaults often could not pay for medical services and were reluctant to seek the help of the police who surveilled and limited free speech in the encampments. In a response reminiscent of early underground rape crisis volunteers, Ivy drew on her feminist consciousness to provide counseling support and raise awareness against sexual harassment and rape. The members of the Safer Spaces Working Group created a boundary between the police, the Occupy movement at large, and participants who actively opposed sexual and gender harassment. They offered solidarity to recipients of gender conflict.

Outrage about gender conflict, women's subordination, and sexual violence against women, and gender and sexual minorities sparked the development of feminist collective identities and solidarity, including consciousness about how to create a "feminist movement culture" (Taylor and Whittier 1995). The meaning of the gender conflicts that plagued the Occupy movement from its inception were intelligible to women who had participated in 1960s' and 1970s' feminist movements, belonged to contemporary feminist organizations, or had taken feminist studies classes in colleges and universities. As a result, feminists were able to use gender conflict as an opportunity to build on and extend existing feminist collective identities. Furthermore, they brought feminist solidarity to bear against gender subordination and oppression within the Occupy movement.

Feminist "Free Spaces"

In addition to developing feminist solidarity to confront male domination and sexual violence, women, transgender, and genderqueer participants formed feminist "free spaces"[7] in which to prevent, impede, and resist gender conflict. Scholars have tended to study free spaces as sites for social movements' emergence; however, prefigurative free spaces can also develop within ongoing movements as sites where participants can express a distinctive collective identity, a utopian way of living, an innovative culture, or mount opposition to the movement overall (Allen 1970; Polletta 1999; Polletta and Kretschmer 2013). Prefigurative free spaces allow participants to mobilize around issues related to their own unique grievances and collective identities. In free spaces, activists create a distinct boundary between themselves and dominant movement actors. Segregated feminist "free spaces" have been a strategy used by feminists to explicitly confront and diffuse gender conflict while forging feminist solidarity (Freedman 1995). In the Occupy movement, feminist "free spaces" served as a base from which participants mobilized feminist support for the movement's goals and strategies. The spaces became a mechanism to promote participation in the larger Occupy movement *and* in feminism. They allowed for the expression of feminism and the prefiguring of a feminist culture. They were spaces dedicated to opposing gender conflict, such as male-dominated gender hierarchies. In these segregated feminist spaces, activists drew on feminist cultures and traditions to develop feminist protest tactics, media, and cultures.

Within the Occupy movement, free spaces took many forms, including meetings and events, roped-off feminist quadrants in the encampments, Facebook pages, email discussion lists, online conference calls, and other online spaces. Feminists created segregated spaces to facilitate the participation of women, genderqueer, and sexual minorities in the movement. In larger encampments, it was not uncommon for feminists to sleep in sex-segregated tents and to designate sectors of encampments for women and members of queer communities. In the Zuccotti Park encampment in New York City, a group of women, transgender, and lesbian and gay participants decided to sleep together overnight in a large army tent designated by the Safer Spaces Working Group as a "safe space" explicitly for women and queer people. Feminists guarded the tent in shifts and spent considerable energy to preserve its safety (Quinn 2011). Similarly, in Oakland, feminist "free spaces" included OOP barbecues and separate feminist areas within the Oakland encampment that nurtured a feminist culture.

Within the spaces, the majority of participants considered themselves feminists. Feminists consciously and continually engaged in maintaining a boundary between the feminist "free spaces" dominated by feminists, women, and queer communities in opposition to spaces that were dominated by heterosexual men. Jessica, a millennial participant in OOP, explains:

Interviewer: When you say a feminist occupation—I'm trying to understand—what made it feminist?
Jessica: What made it feminist? It was organized by feminists so that it would be an autonomous space for women and

> queer people and trans folks. That was always the thing—
> it was always a little bit unclear, but by and large, it was a
> space without many hetero cis men, if any.
> Interviewer: Was that ever defined by the group—that this is
> the place for people who do not identify as hetero cis men?
> Jessica: No—and sometimes. I actually feel like I'm oversim-
> plifying. But I think the point was that it was not about
> making rules that people had to follow. It was about creat-
> ing a culture.

Jessica further explained that segregated zones for feminists, especially women and queer people, became sites where a feminist culture flourished. They provided safe spaces for feminists and gender
and sexual minorities by limiting the participation of "hetero cis
men"—in other words, men who are assigned male at birth, who have
embraced male and heterosexual identities, and who typically enjoy
privilege on the basis of their dominant gender and sexual identities.
By reducing the involvement of hetero cis men, the space provided an
opportunity for straight or queer women, lesbians, gay men, transgender persons, and other gender and sexual minorities to embrace
feminist culture and participate fully in the Occupy movement. The
feminist culture that participants created was otherwise absent and
submerged in other parts of the encampments and the main movement's organizations. In Occupy Oakland, the feminist "free space,"
for example, embraced radical anti-patriarchal, anti-racist, and anti-
homophobic politics. Segregated feminist "free spaces" were online
and offline sites controlled by women, queer people, and feminist
participants who sought refuge from a movement that often appeared
to be dominated by white men. They were also places in which to
mount challenges to the male-dominated culture.

Feminist "free spaces" allowed feminist participants to organize
events separate from the main Occupy organizations. At these events,
they promoted feminist objectives as well as the goals of the Occupy
movement. Exemplary are the FemGAs. WOWS and the FemGA
group held four assemblies in New York City between May 17 and
August 18, 2012. Each New York City FemGA had a different theme
to encourage a diversity of participation, including the definition
of feminism, LGBTQ issues, and the interests of people of color. In

addition, the first national FemGA took place at NatGat in July 2012. Occupy groups in Boston, Chicago, Los Angeles, and a handful of small towns held similar gatherings. These events often followed a format advertised as a "tool kit" on http://www.womenoccupy.org. The majority of FemGA attendees practiced consciousness raising, a tactical innovation of 1960s' and 1970s' feminists (Freeman 1975). In feminist "free spaces," feminists participated in the larger movement and drew feminists from beyond the Occupy movement into it.

Feminist "free spaces" created feminist segregation within the Occupy movement. Segregated free spaces allow feminists to form boundaries that set them apart from male-dominated groups and networks (Freedman 1995). In these separate bases of support for feminism, participants have the autonomy to embrace feminist politics, tactics, practices, and leadership styles (Taylor and Rupp 1993; Taylor and Whittier 1992). While feminist "free spaces" within the Occupy movement were initially a response to the white male domination of the main organizations and to the gender conflict that plagued them, ultimately they became opportunities for feminists to form solidarity, promote feminist consciousness, and practice feminist politics.

Feminist Bridge Leaders

Gender conflict and white male dominance in the main Occupy organizations contributed to the marginalization of feminists and gender and sexual minorities. This resulted in a leadership hierarchy dominated mainly by white men. Like other "leaderless" movements that practice participatory democracy, Occupy was subject to latent and persistent status hierarchies based on ability and identity (Freeman 1975; Leach 2013; Polletta 2002). As a result, women found limited opportunities for leadership in the larger movement. Instead, feminists served primarily as grassroots and informal leaders, or what Belinda Robnett (1997) describes in her study of the civil rights movement as "bridge leaders." Women were not legitimated by a formal leadership structure or by other movement leaders. Neither followers nor the movement's targets recognized women's or genderqueer persons' leadership. Women worked for the movement primarily as bridge leaders, connecting feminist, queer, and racial and sexual minority communities to Occupy.

Although many of the general assemblies, occupations, and protest events were led and dominated by white men, the outcome of these events often depended on women leaders' ability to mobilize grassroots participation. Esther, who participated in the planning of key marches and protest events on October 5 and November 17, 2011, epitomizes a strong leader and organizer who was marginalized because of her gender. She recounts the sexism she confronted at a meeting to plan the November 17 protest:

> I saw that people were being really dismissive and really doubtful of everything that I was saying, but I was the one who had been on the phone and who had been doing all the work. And at one point, I looked around, and I realized I was the only woman, and I was like, "We need more women here." And I felt like I was being silenced, and it led to this discussion happening right there on the spot that was very unsafe for me. I was the only woman, and I started crying. At one point, this one guy was like, "I feel like you're silencing me, because you're talking too much." And someone else was like, "She's the one doing the work!"

Esther explains that her contributions to the movement were undermined by other mainly male participants because she was not taken seriously as a woman. Although she was an effective organizer, as the only woman who attended many organizing meetings, she was subjected to sexism and made to feel like an outcast.

Likewise, Derby was constrained by male-dominated leadership and a male hierarchy in decision making about protests. Derby expresses frustration over being excluded by the movement's male-dominated leadership, explaining that the only leadership opportunities open to her and other women were as bridge leaders:

> It's so dumb—when you want to get anything done, there's a white guy somewhere that you need to talk to. The two guys that ran [a particular protest-planning group] kept telling me it had to be a small group of people, [but in actuality] I wasn't put on this committee because of those dudes, who didn't work with women. They just didn't. And I was told by those dudes

that the movement had to grow and accommodate for these different ways that decisions were made, that we couldn't do everything through consensus.

Although Derby was an experienced organizer, a formal leader in other movements, and a student leader at her university, she was excluded from the formal leadership of the protest-planning group. Esther and Derby exemplify the experience of bridge leaders who were marginalized and denied formal leadership status. They had to struggle to take part in meetings about the movement's strategy and tactics and were never treated as legitimate leaders, even though they contributed extensively to grassroots mobilization.

While many women, queer people, people of color, and feminists may have been formal leaders in other institutions (such as in schools or workplaces) or in other social movements, in the context of the Occupy movement, they became mainly grassroots and informal leaders. Kite, a participant in progressive, lesbian, and feminist communities in the eastern United States, observes: "It was almost like a service capacity thing that women were doing [as meeting facilitators], rather than I think one that shaped an agenda." According to Kite, women participated in and performed tasks during meetings, such as organizing speakers. However, the majority of women were not permitted to structure the meetings or hold leadership roles in the main movement's organizations. Family commitments also deterred Kite from consistently sleeping at the encampments, which illustrates the extent to which the movement's key tactic—encampments—by its very nature tended to exclude women and others with family responsibilities (see also Calhoun 2013 for a critical evaluation of encampments as limiting the potential of the movement). Kite had held formal leadership roles in lesbian and feminist organizations and was a key force in recruiting members of these constituencies to participate in the Occupy movement. However, she became a bridge leader and did not assume formal leadership responsibilities in the Occupy movement because of participants' tokenization of women and view of women as illegitimate leaders.

Although excluded from formal leadership, bridge leaders' access to the resources and memberships of preexisting local and national organizations and networks allowed them to function as key grassroots leaders. For example, Jade worked extensively with a national feminist organization and assumed a bridge leader role in the Occupy movement, concentrating on grassroots organizing in her local community. She explains why she did not seek a formal leadership position in the Occupy movement: "I'm a lifetime local organizer, and I was like, 'I don't live in that community [in New York City], I live in another smaller community in another state.' So then I came back, and I started an Occupy in my local neighborhood." Furthermore, Laura explains the kind of grassroots leadership and organizing that many women engaged in to connect women, lesbian, gay, bisexual, and transgender activist networks to the Occupy movement in the San Francisco Bay Area: "I helped mother the Occupy Pride [by finding them meeting space] and helped mother the SF Women's Alliance." Laura uses the term "mother" to describe how she used her relationships as a feminist bridge leader to connect groups focused on gender and sexuality to mobilize for Occupy. Feminist bridge leaders drew on resources from feminist mobilizing structures created by generations of feminists who had been active in 1960s', 1970s', and contemporary feminist mobilizations. As these participants' stories suggest, feminist bridge leaders expanded the Occupy movement's base of support.

This analysis extends Robnett's (1997) term "bridge leaders" to examine one of the ways in which gender conflict contributes to the persistence of feminism. Like bridge leaders in the civil rights movement, bridge leaders in the Occupy movement emerged as a consequence of women's marginalization and exclusion from a leadership hierarchy dominated by men. Although women bridge leaders were formal leaders in other institutional settings and in other movements, their opportunities for leadership in the context of the Occupy movement were mainly as grassroots and informal leaders.

Conclusion

Persistent gender conflict sparked feminist mobilization within the Occupy movement. Women and genderqueer persons of many races and ethnicities acted swiftly—much more quickly than in prior generations—to critique sexism and white male dominance in many of the movement's spaces. An extensive cadre of feminists from 1960s' and 1970s' to contemporary movements worked together to respond to gender conflict. They brought preexisting feminist and women's movements into coalition with the Occupy movement, and they developed new explicitly feminist organizations. By nurturing a feminist collective identity, feminist "free spaces," and feminist bridge leaders, they challenged gender inequality and other forms of oppression within the movement. Feminist activists, many of whom shaped their political consciousness around a politics of intersectionality (P. Collins and Bilge 2016; Tormos 2017), achieved intersectional praxis and contributed simultaneously to feminism and the Occupy movement. The experiences of feminist participants within the Occupy movement demonstrate best practices to answer this research question: How did Occupy movement participants build solidarity across gender, race, class, and sexual identities within the mass movement? This chapter provides a case study of the processes that can mobilize feminism even within not-explicitly feminist organizations.

Even though the Occupy movement provided an opportunity for contemporary feminist activism, it was neither a feminist movement nor solely an incidence of anti-feminist backlash (Faludi 2006; Reger 2012; Staggenborg and Taylor 2005). Some scholars and journalists argue that women participated in all aspects of the movement's work and that feminist organizations contributed significantly to the Occupy protests (Brunner 2011; Maharawal 2011; Milkman, Luce, and Lewis 2013; Seltzer 2011; Stevens 2011). Others argue that the Occupy movement was dominated by white men, that sexism was rampant but ignored in the encampments and in movement organizations, and that feminism was peripheral to the movement (M. Butler 2011; Eschele 2016; McVeigh 2011; Pickerill and Krinsky 2012; Reger 2015). I view this debate as symptomatic of the current state of feminism, which Jo Reger (2012) characterizes as "nowhere-everywhere," meaning that feminist beliefs and protests simultaneously appear trivial and "dead" or "nowhere" and yet persist among women as a basis of identity, solidarity, and mobilization. Findings suggest that women and genderqueer persons participated significantly in the Occupy movement but also that conflict mitigated their contributions.

Even though Reger develops the theory of "nowhere-everywhere feminism" by examining explicitly feminist communities, "nowhere-everywhere" characterizes tensions about feminism within the

Occupy movement as well. "Nowhere" feminism (Reger 2012) in the Occupy movement took the forms of sexism and anti-feminist practices, such as the absence of intersectionality; the subordination of women, genderqueer persons, and sexual minorities in meetings or interviews with the press; and sometimes even sexual harassment and rape. Yet "everywhere" feminism (Reger 2012) thrived within the Occupy movement as well in the forms of its ideals for diversity and inclusivity, infighting about intersectional analyses of inequalities, and the wide participation of women, feminists, queer people, and sexual minorities who advocated for feminist issues within the movement. It is necessary to examine more systematically the persistence of gender conflict *and* feminist mobilization within existing social movements to uncover the processes that feminists can deploy to implement intersectional praxis.

Conclusion

Intersectionality Lessons for Mass Movements

The Occupy movement called hundreds of thousands of Americans into the streets to protest rising economic inequality and advocate for greater democracy. Inspired by activists in Greece, Spain, Egypt, Tunisia, several additional Arab countries, and Wisconsin, the Occupy movement adopted the encampment tactic. The movement spread from New York City, to San Francisco, to more than one thousand town squares around the United States and the world. With the mushrooming of encampments, the Occupy movement activated the contemporary period of protest (Calhoun 2013). Complementing the face-to-face protests, activists developed innovative online networks. It was the first mass movement in the United States to extensively utilize social media. Furthermore, newly politicized millennials who had recently graduated from college but were underemployed handled much of the online organizing (Milkman 2017).

The slogan "We are the 99%" became a powerful new way to conceptualize inequality. Framing the Occupy movement as being about the 99% versus the 1% deepened Americans' awareness of economic inequality (Calhoun 2013; Morin 2012). The movement sparked novel widespread discussion in the American media about inequality (Calhoun 2013; Gaby and Caren 2016). Participants attempted to design the movement's organizational structure to match its goal for equality. They built a nonhierarchical and egalitarian structure, aiming to create a radically inclusive movement. Research has celebrated the movement as the first diffusion of a consensus-based "structurelessness" participatory democracy movement in the United States in decades (Piven 2013). Women, men, and genderqueer persons worked together in a number of mixed-gender and racially diverse groups within the movement.

The movement grew quickly in New York City and the San Francisco Bay Area. But activists did not adequately train each other how to distribute tasks equitably among men, women, and genderqueer persons of many different races, ethnicities, class backgrounds, and sexual orientations. Due to the structurelessness of the movement, leaders neither managed how participants worked in groups nor evaluated the effectiveness of these teams. The movement mirrored the limited equality that scholars Maria Charles and Karen Bradley (2002, 2009) characterize as "equal opportunity individualism." Similar to girls who tend to study the humanities while boys tend to study math and engineering (Charles and Bradley 2002, 2009; Correll 2004), participants in Occupy chose to accomplish activities based on their individual beliefs about his/her/their identities and what someone of his/her/their identities should do. Furthermore, participants held each other to deeply rooted cultural expectations about appropriate gender, race, class, and sexual expressions. Within the rapidly growing progressive movement, the acceptance of individualism and traditional beliefs about identity led to participants re-creating traditional hierarchies.

Among activists and in the media, participants debated enthusiastically about the movement's dynamics and strategies. Some participants critiqued the Occupy movement's uneven gender composition and the lack of racial and sexual diversity. Individuals who joined the Occupy movement expected their voices to be represented in its analysis. But those who identified as female, people of color, and/or queer reported being marginalized by white and/or male participants. Despite joining a mass movement that claimed to be for the 99%, many women endured harassment and limited leadership opportunities. Feminists encountered resistance to their ideas and practices. Whether and how the movement did or should incorporate feminist politics was a constant struggle.

Prior studies of the Occupy movement have tended to analyze the conflicts that plagued the movement through a lens that ignores the race, gender, class, and sexuality dimensions of the movement (Leach 2013; Lewis and Luce 2012; Schneider 2013; J. Smith and Glidden 2012). Instead, I intersectionally analyze the movement's dynamics and culture by asking the following questions: How did Occupy movement participants build solidarity across gender, race, class, and sexual identities within the mass movement? Under what conditions do movement cultures exclude or alienate particular individuals and groups? How do gender, race, class, and sexuality processes influence contemporary social movement dynamics and culture? With this study, I join a range of feminist scholars who intersectionally study the emergence, development, and decline of social movements (for example, Beckwith 1996; Blee 2002; Carastathis 2016; Choo and Ferree 2010; P. Collins and Bilge 2016; Eschle 2016; Irvine, Lang, and Montoya 2019; Laperrière and Lépinard 2016; Robnett 1997; B. Roth 2004, 2017; Rupp and Taylor 2003; Taylor 1999; Terriquez 2015; Townsend-Bell 2011). I conclude by revisiting how the Occupy movement's collective identities, frames, leadership, and forms of feminism fulfilled the intersectional imperative or engaged in other forms of analysis and praxis. Then, I analyze how the Occupy movement has continued, transformed, and influenced contemporary politics. Finally, I suggest lessons to improve future contemporary social movements.

Fault Lines within the 99%

The majority of participants with whom I spoke believed that gender hierarchies *and* gender egalitarianism structured the movement. Informal hierarchies privileged white elite men. Some participants recognized that sex segregation and the gendered division of labor were problematic. Racism, discrimination against queer people and sexual minorities, and class-based inequalities exacerbated gender conflict. Some participants challenged powerful structures of inequality, while others fell back on re-creating traditional gender, race, sexual, and class hierarchies. Participants inconsistently deployed strategies to address sexism and racism. Conflict over the lack of diversity in the movement's collective identities, frames, and leadership sparked conflicts that contributed to its fading.

An extensive network of oppositional groups flourished within the Occupy movement, contributing to its vibrancy and complexity. As individuals broke off into subcommittees, the creative, critical, innovative, and diverse ideas that energize mobilization flowed away from the main movement. Rather than resolve fissures, leaders in the main movement's organizations tacitly accepted the conflicts posed by such groups as Decolonize, the Speakeasy Caucus, Queering OWS [Occupy Wall Street], and the twenty-four-seven Occupiers. Participants in these groups and others who believed that their experiences were not represented in the main movement's organizations developed oppositional collective identities. While critiquing the Occupy identity, the groups maintained the participation of gender, race, sexual, and class minorities. They opposed the 99% identity and yet continued to contribute to the mass mobilization.

The separation of groups with oppositional collective identities from the main movement's organizations allowed participants to evade the conflicts. Keeping conflicts away from the main movement diluted infighting, but new social-media technologies facilitated the airing of grievances rapidly and unceasingly, which contributed to separatism. The presence of "color-blind racism" (Beeman 2015; Bonilla-Silva 2006) alongside "racism-evasiveness" strategies (Beeman 2015) indicated the movement's uneven commitment to ending racism and also sparked the development of oppositional collective identities focused on racial justice. The marginalization of sexual minorities; debates about whether to celebrate lesbian, gay, bisexual, transgender, and queer/questioning (LGBTQ) rights as a part of the mass movement; and the prominence of heteronormativity alienated queer participants, who then developed separate LGBTQ organizations and tactics. Despite the Occupy movement's co-occurrence with the shift to the legalization of same-sex marriage in the United States, the most widespread and radical transformation of public opinion about LGBTQ issues in the history of the country, its leaders did not develop strong coalitions with members of LGBTQ movements. Furthermore, by prioritizing the 99% identity, many Occupy participants glossed over class diversity. The analysis of class inequality as being "everyone except the 1%" erased participants' distinct experiences of poverty that warranted greater attention than just a focus on regulating big banks. Online activism complemented face-to-face contact and invigorated solidarity among the new subgroups. The loose structure of the mass movement provided an opportunity for oppositional groups to separate and for the main groups to accept this separatism. Volunteer-driven, unregulated committees proliferated within the Occupy movement (Montoya 2019), splintering the movement when it did not significantly modify the 99% collective identity to be more inclusive.

Although the 99% collective identity signaled an opportunity for solidarity, it was an insufficient frame for inclusivity within a mass movement. Participants deployed three main inclusivity frames, which each signaled the inclusion of particular people. Although the 99% frame attracted a range of activists to the mass movement, it was not explicitly intersectional. Media and culture framed as being for the 99% only broadly and vaguely conveyed messages of "everyone's included," usually alongside the underlying message to "do whatever you want." The individualism embedded in the 99% frame detracted from opportunities to build connections across people of diverse identities. The 99% frame indicated inclusion for those affected by class inequality. Nevertheless, for participants whose existence lay at the intersection of two or more structures of inequality, the movement failed to explicitly call for their necessary participation, let alone recognize their grievances. The need for frames that more specifically analyzed inequality intersectionally led to fragmentation. Dominance frames also reinforced fractures within the movement about how white people and men controlled its culture. Media and cultural products that signaled the inclusion of privileged white men's ideas, bodies, emotions, and cultures excluded representations of and issues important to women of many races and ethnicities. Yet still other frames utilized an intersectional lens by representing the stories and experiences of women and queer protesters. Media and cultural products that utilized an intersectional frame analyzed class inequalities as being interlinked with other structures of inequality. Participants who intersectionally represented inequalities created media and culture that sparked opportunities for coalitions, especially with racial justice, LGBTQ, and feminist movements, and accomplished the intersectional imperative.

Still, men were more likely to participate in high-risk tactics, sleep in the encampments, and participate in decision-making and leadership activities. Such practices as all-night encampments in urban centers, mic checks where the loudest and boldest were the most heard, and a voluntary and unregulated leadership structure prioritized men's participation and marginalized women, queer people, and people of color.

Within any organizational structure, leaders cannot accomplish their responsibilities without followers. Followers provide vital feedback to leaders. Particularly active, engaged followers can also help leaders steer the organization toward meeting its collective goals. In the Occupy movement, the prevailing ethos was "leaderlessness" and "horizontalism," ideologies intended to distribute responsibility for leadership tasks to many different participants and empower a range of leaders and followers. Yet in practice, followers were more likely to recognize white people and/or men as leaders. Followers conditioned whether women and queer people were considered legitimate leaders. Followers demonstrated their lack of support for women and queer bottom-liners and facilitators by performing discriminatory resistance. Forms of discriminatory resistance within the Occupy movement were similar to barriers to leadership in hierarchical contexts, including holding women leaders to the double bind, harassment, male dominance, and the development of a hostile culture. Many women became token rather than legitimate leaders.

Yet feminist participants recognized sexism, racism, classism, and discrimination based on sexuality early in the development of the movement. Familiar with critiquing inequality, feminists saw opportunities for mobilization in the Occupy movement. Hopeful that the Occupy movement could renew mass activism, activists from established feminist organizations contributed resources. Participants brought a range of feminist politics to the movement, from prioritizing the voices and experiences of women of color, to developing queer and intersectional feminisms, to celebrating trans women who led feminist organizing.

As a response to infighting and the limited opportunities for women and queer leaders, feminists created their own feminist collective identities, feminist "free spaces," and feminist bridge leaders. They contributed to the momentum of Occupy and even furthered feminism from within the mixed-gender and sometimes anti-feminist movement. Many millennials, queer participants, and feminists engaged in cutting-edge debates about contemporary feminism and intersectional analysis. These feminists produced tactics, strategies, and goals exemplary of the intersectional imperative. Internal movement conflicts became nascent opportunities for intersectional activism *and* led to the Occupy movement's transformation and demobilization.

Studies of social movements have paid significant attention to the ways in which infighting and debates over goals, framing, and collective identity influence social movements' development (see, for example, Bernstein and Taylor 2013; W. Gamson 1975; Ghaziani 2008). Conflicts over gender and sexuality issues, racism, and class inequality are additional crucial areas of infighting and debate that have yet to receive significant attention (exceptions include, for example, Evans 1979; B. Roth 2004, 2017; and, for a review, Hurwitz and Crossley 2019). Central to the Occupy movement's emergence, development, fading, and dispersion into a variety of new forms of activism were debates about the lack of intersectional praxis.

What Happened to Occupy?

Despite the fault lines within the Occupy movement, many individuals learned how to organize and protest together. They developed new political consciousness or renewed their commitments to social justice by participating in the movement. They practiced such tactics as encampments, street theater, and live Tweeting. They marched and performed acts of civil disobedience. They organized by posting, friending other participants, and creating events on Facebook. Each of the tactics and strategies that activists developed during the Occupy movement became skills for developing subsequent mobilizations.

A thousand impassioned protesters assembled in a park in New York City, holding signs bearing the slogans "Tax the R1%CH," "Power to the 99%," and "Join the Revolution," the latter of which was embellished with the image of a Guy Fawkes[1] mask. After several speeches decrying corporate executives' and Wall Street bankers' greed, the protesters marched, filling a lane of Broadway stretching at least a quarter mile. As they wound their way downtown, they chanted, "Hey hey, ho ho, corporate greed has got to go." When they landed in Zuccotti Park, a few blocks from the New York Stock Exchange, they shouted, "We. Are. The 99%!" Yet this event did not take place in the fall of 2011 during the birth of the Occupy movement; it was a January 30, 2016, demonstration organized by the group Millennials for Bernie [Sanders]. Many of the individuals who had actively participated in Occupy encampments and committees brought this knowledge to other social movement groups from 2012 to 2016, including many in support of Bernie Sanders's 2015 to 2016 presidential campaign. Evidenced by the breadth and strength of the Sanders campaign, the Occupy movement persisted and transformed through a period of abeyance (Taylor 1989).

Sanders's campaign brought about a new phase of the Occupy movement focused not on the development of leaderless encampments but instead on winning the highest elected leadership position in the federal government. A group of millennials who were too young to participate in the Occupy movement learned about economic justice and challenging the 1% by joining with Sanders.

Both Occupy participants and Sanders conveyed political messages that critiqued the inordinate wealth and power of corporations. Both movements advocated economic stability for the majority of Americans. Sanders refused campaign contributions from billionaire funders. Occupiers who were still running traditional and online media contributed to mobilizing for Sanders. *The Occupied Wall Street Journal*, a movement newspaper published by Occupy supporters from 2011 to 2012, published a special issue to support Sanders in the New York primaries. Furthermore, social media networks developed by Occupy participants in 2011 and 2012 became mobilizing structures of support for Sanders's campaign. Those Facebook networks persisted from 2012 through at least 2016.[2] The slogan "Bernie Sanders: Not for Sale" encapsulated the senator's solidarity with the 99%. His campaign breathed new life into the Occupy movement.

Occupy and Bernie activism were also similar because each weathered conflicts about issues related to feminism, women, LGBTQ persons, and racial justice. For example, in 2016, on the television show *Real Time with Bill Maher*, feminist leader Gloria Steinem promoted Sanders's competitor for the Democratic nomination, Hillary Clinton, and also criticized millennial women who were supporting candidates other than Clinton. She reasoned that they participated in Sanders's activism because, "When you're young, you're thinking, where are the boys? The boys are with Bernie." Her surprisingly sexist comment sparked #NotHereForBoys, hashtag activism symbolizing women's and feminists' legitimate support for Sanders's platform.

Implicit in Steinem's critique was the stereotype that Sanders's activists were all white and male, or "Bernie Bros" (Hess 2016). Debates about how to include feminism within Sanders's activism and whether white men dominated the movement were persistent. Using social media, the group Women for Bernie Sanders mobilized a series of grassroots-coordinated meetups on International Women's Day, March 8, 2016, to build solidarity among women and strengthen women's participation in Sanders's mobilizations. Yet many women supporters of the Democratic Party joined Clinton's explicitly feminist campaign, which focused on electing the first woman president of the United States. Despite the support of many women and feminists, Sanders's activists struggled to build an intersectional movement that could appeal to baby boomer feminists.

Even though the media spotlight on the Occupy movement had dimmed by mid-2012, the movement continued nationally in the form of Sanders's presidential campaign and locally through a variety of grassroots organizations. Changing political opportunities external to the movement, disagreements over its goals and strategies, and conflicts related to the lack of intersectional praxis within it motivated activists to strengthen the oppositional collective identities they had formed as a part of the Occupy mobilizations. Many of the groups that developed oppositional collective identities from within the Occupy movement became independent organizations. Many also shifted their energies into movements other than the Occupy movement.

Across the country, participants from the Occupy movement developed new but related movements. By meeting each other in the encampments, activists formed new networks. They discovered shared grievances and developed new organizations to address those concerns. Many organizations brought together new objectives with Occupy tactics or collective identities. From 2011 onward, Occupy Our Homes became a force in the housing rights movements in Minnesota and Atlanta (Manilov 2013). In 2012, Occupiers in New York City created Occupy Sandy in response to the Hurricane Sandy disaster. Local residents and even the Red Cross relied on Occupiers for emergency food and hygiene products. The effort was so effective because Occupiers had preexisting online and offline mobilizing structures in place for how to build temporary communities, acquire donations, feed thousands of people, and mobilize hundreds of volunteers. Also in 2012, a short drive from Occupy Oakland (OO), Occupiers developed an urban community farm project, "Occupy the Farm," on an underused piece of University of California land in Berkeley. They extended the momentum for Occupy encampments but addressed food insecurity and environmental issues along with economic inequality. Another group to spawn from the Occupy movement in 2012 was Strike Debt. Celebrated as an attempt to take some authority away from banks, Strike Debt became an online and face-to-face "people's collection agency" (Piven 2014). To address economic inequality using a novel tactic, they bought and expunged the medical debts of those living in impoverished zip codes. In addition, some education and protest groups remained active from 2011 through 2016. The San Francisco Occupy Forum and the Alternative Banking Working Group in New York continued to meet weekly through at least 2016. This list is not exhaustive; these are a few of the many groups that persisted beyond the destruction of the encampments in the fall of 2011. The Occupy movement's mass organizing and its internal fault lines opened political opportunities for many more mobilizations.

A little more than a year after most of the Occupy demonstrations had shifted into less public forms of organizing, three queer black women initiated Black Lives Matter, a renewed contemporary civil rights movement. Although the movement grew out of racial justice organizing, Black Twitter,[3] and other social media organizing, several key mobilizations within the Occupy movement contributed to the newly recharged national mobilizations against police brutality. The Decolonize movement fought racism among progressive activists and demonstrated the need for black-person-led movements. Hoodie marches and anti-stop-and-frisk actions organized through Inter-Occupy's website and other social media expanded public critique against stand-your-ground laws and excessive and racially targeted policing. Many former Occupy participants welcomed the Black Lives Matter movement, which prioritized the experiences of people of color and drew on intersectional analyses about the need for racial, gender, sexuality, and class equality.[4] Future research should examine more fully the connections between the Occupy movement and Black Lives Matter and compare and contrast each movement's use or lack of intersectional praxis.

In the early 2010s, feminists contributed to the Occupy movement; by the mid- to late 2010s, they had shifted their energies into a resurgence of visible mass feminist activism. Feminist movements, such as the Women's March and Me Too, anchored the resistance to Donald Trump's presidential administration. In her study of contemporary feminists on college campuses, Alison Dahl Crossley (2017) finds that contemporary feminists do not believe the idea of waves or the "third wave" to be useful. Drawing on these data, she argues for "waveless feminism," comparing the life course of social movements to rivers and "emphasiz[ing] the persistence of feminism over time" (20). To persist for so long and to address so many diverse goals, feminist movements have evolved into a variety of new organizational contexts (Staggenborg and Taylor 2005). Contemporary feminism spills over into contemporary social movements, influencing new not-explicitly feminist movements and feminism itself (Hurwitz 2019; Meyer and Whittier 1994). Feminist contributions to the Occupy movement and feminist-centered organizing like the Women's March support Crossley's analysis of feminism as "river-like"—long-lasting, sometimes surging, sometimes gurgling along, but constantly flowing to influence social movements in the United States and globally.

The Occupy movement renewed hope in mass street demonstrations in the United States. After Occupy, individuals and groups in the wider progressive community contributed to Black Lives Matter; feminist movements; the Fight for $15, focused on unionizing and raising fast-food workers' wages to $15 per hour; the climate justice movement; electrifying civil disobedience led by indigenous activists against transporting oil through the Dakota Access Pipeline; demonstrations against President Trump's white supremacy and sexism; the student-led gun-control March For Our Lives movement; and much more. Although each of these movements has its own history of emergence, particular goals, and dynamics, many people who participated in Occupy have also supported these movements online and during face-to-face demonstrations.

Furthermore, the U.S. and global Occupy movement inspired pro-democracy protests worldwide that incorporated the encampment tactic. In June 2013, activists in Istanbul protested a government plan to destroy Gezi Park and replace it with a shopping mall. For two weeks, they slept, ate, and shared art, stories, and humor as they occupied the park (Arat 2019). The Gezi Park encampment also became a political opportunity for the continuation of Turkey's women's movements (Arat 2019). Feminists contributed significantly to the Gezi protests. Some women engaged in high-risk demonstrations that electrified the nation, including "the woman in red." Police pepper-sprayed a woman wearing a red dress. Her photo spread quickly through Turkish and international media. She came to represent the lively, bold spirit of Gezi protesters in opposition to government control (Arat 2019). However, like Occupiers who criticized gender conflict within the movement, Turkish feminists consistently critiqued stereotypical gender expectations that threatened to sideline women's activism. Women's forums separated from the main movement due to men dominating opportunities to speak (Arat 2019). In Hong Kong, from 2013 through 2014 and beyond, Occupy Central with Peace and Love emerged. Known for their use of bright yellow umbrellas during their occupations and acts of civil disobedience, participants advocated for democracy for the people of Hong Kong against control by mainland China (Jacobs 2016). A few years later and halfway across the world, in March 2016, students and labor unions joined in France to protest precarious labor conditions for young workers. The movement became known as Nuit Debout (Up all Night), because its participants occupied public squares day and night for several weeks (Pickard and Bessant 2018). The initial occupation of a public square in Paris inspired solidarity actions in smaller cities across the country. Like the Occupy movement, Nuit Debout participants largely organized the movement on social media and practiced horizontalism.

These examples are just a few of the global extensions of the Occupy movement. Each movement is a part of a cycle of protest popularized by the Occupy movement that employed the encampment tactic, pro-democracy goals, horizontalism, and creative use of social media. Still, from the Arab Uprisings, to the 15-M/Indignados movement in Spain, to Occupy, to Gezi, each of these progressive, pro-democracy protests of the contemporary period has been limited by discrimination against women, queer people, and/or racial minorities (Arat 2019; Hafez 2014; López and García 2014; Salime 2012). Creating inclusive, mass, effective movements that engage in intersectional praxis remains a challenge (Carastathis 2016; Irvine, Lang, and Montoya 2019). Contemporary social movements must address the intersecting structures of inequality that allow individuals to act with either relative freedom or limitations within social movements and in society broadly.

Intersectionality Lessons

Throughout this study, in their own words, Occupy protesters have revealed how a social movement that aimed to create equality fell back on traditional gender, racial, sexual, and class hierarchies. Traditionally marginalized persons, especially women and queer people of a variety of races and ethnicities, provoked a radical education among their peers about intersectionality. These cases of intersectional praxis—and the lack of intersectional praxis—provide models and warnings for contemporary activists who aspire to build unity across race, class, gender, and sexual differences. Future progressive contemporary movements depend on learning lessons about the achievements and mistakes in the Occupy movement.

Organizing a mass movement necessitates intersectionally analyzing the problems that affect groups of potential participants. Gendered, raced, classed, and sexual systems of power and privilege are intertwined. Activists who practice the intersectional imperative fulfill three criteria: (1) they address multiple forms of inequality with specificity, (2) they depict the lives and stories of people who are multiply marginalized, and (3) they encourage coalition building with other groups and movements from outside the main movement. Mass movements must mediate between and across intersectional identities. To produce sustainable, viable movements that involve a large number of people, participants must engage in coalition building across identities and beyond the contours of the initial mass movement. The intersectional imperative generates intersectional praxis; it is an intention for inclusivity across diverse people. As activists form collective identities, media and culture, leadership, and feminist organizing, they can model an inclusive prefigurative society by relying on the intersectional imperative as a moral compass. Furthermore, progressive left-leaning movements can initiate coalition building by embracing the principles of the intersectional imperative. This study suggests that social movements attract more diverse memberships, quell internal conflicts, and develop prefigurative movements that seek to end all inequalities when participants utilize intersectional praxis.

"Big-tent" mass movements are special social institutions. They are unlike movements focused on one or a few related issues (such as animal rights movements or student movements). Mass movements intend to find commonalities across a wide range of the population. Therefore, if social movement participants begin to develop oppositional collective identities within a mass movement, the main movement's organizations must respond to conflicts and should act to rebuild cohesion. When oppositional collective identities that critique monist analyses of a movement emerge, participants should stop driving the movement forward and instead slow down to do the difficult work of modifying its collective identity. The main movement's leaders may need to reframe the boundaries of inclusivity as the mass movement develops. In the case of the Occupy movement, the evasion of conflicts about oppositional collective identities soured the mass mobilization. Individuals left the main movement's organizations feeling frustration and exclusion. Future social movements must find ways to create nimble collective identities within the main movements and empower leaders to shift their frames, goals, and collective identities in response to thoughtful intersectional critiques.

The ethos of a leaderless movement does not take into account how easily followers default to traditional, enduring, unequal power structures. When they practiced "step-up and step-back," Occupy participants attempted to create a leadership structure mindful of intersectional structures of inequality. Future mass movements should train and require leaders to use the step-up and step-back practice. Instead of fostering leaderless movements that place the onus on individuals to volunteer for leadership, social movement activists should manage equal distribution of leadership across people of diverse identities. Mass movements can mitigate discriminatory resistance with leadership trainings and quotas to empower typically marginalized participants to lead. Also necessary are trainings about inequalities in leadership. Leadership theorists in social movement studies should continue interdisciplinary dialogue with scholars in other fields on the cutting edge of leadership studies, including feminist, organizational behavior, and management scholars. Barriers to women's and racial minorities' leadership persist not only in corporate boardrooms but also in social movement organizations.

The Occupy movement's leadership structure and ethos were fragile because there were no formal leaders, no central control over the media and messages, no policing of some of the worst of citizen journalism, little conflict resolution of the tensions that led to the emergence of oppositional collective identities, and it grew so rapidly. Too much of the movement was left to well-intentioned enthusiastic volunteers without proper training. As a result of this loose structure, the movement ostracized many experienced, older women and people of color leaders, the precise leadership base that had been through many intersectional conflicts over decades of progressive activism. Incredible generations of social movement activists have come into political consciousness since the 1960s. The current period is a unique moment in the life of social movements, because activists from the world-shaking decolonization and counterculture movements of the 1960s and 1970s remain active alongside the fervent, technology-savvy, younger generations who have come more recently into political consciousness. Problems with leadership stem not from a lack of a diverse options for who can lead but from ingrained cultural beliefs that limit who are accepted as legitimate leaders.

Across organizational contexts, even beyond social movements, the majority of leaders are white men, and most media are informed by the history of white men's writing and voices. Women of color leaders have been on the front lines, globally advocating for intersectionality, analyzing complex and multiple inequalities, and conceptualizing how to transform social movements (Cho, Crenshaw, and McCall 2013; P. Collins and Bilge 2016; Irvine, Lang, and Montoya 2019). Critiquing organizations in which the majority of leaders are white and/or male raises awareness about white supremacy and the patriarchy. Movements must continue to expose the moral ineptitude and injustice of President Trump, someone who represents the worst of the 1%. Yet anti-1% narratives, rooted in the white male–dominated culture of the U.S. government, are insufficient for building a sustained and inclusive movement. By learning the lessons of the Occupy movement, a mass movement against the Trump administration should be fruitful by prioritizing the intersectional identities, multiple and overlapping grievances, and coalition building with preexisting social movements. Groups that flooded New York airports to protest "the Muslim ban" or the interfaith groups, the Antifa movement, and the civil rights movements that joined together in Charlottesville in 2016 to oppose white-supremacy demonstrations represent ways to use intersectional frames that target not only the wrongs of the 1% but the racial, economic, and national dimensions of the Trump administration's policies.

Even activists within not-explicitly feminist social movements benefit from feminism. Infighting about feminism helped shape the Occupy movement's emergence and development. Future social movements may benefit from the processes that mobilize feminism within not-explicitly feminist social movements and organizational contexts. Future social movements should value the creation of feminist collective identities, feminist "free spaces," and feminist bridge leaders that contribute to mass social movements and spark intersectional praxis while at the same time advancing feminism.

Participants in future social movements should aim to prevent the exit of feminists from their movements and instead work to integrate the major resources that many feminists bring to such groups, including experienced personnel, conscious intersectional politics, and coalition building with a wide variety of preexisting feminist organizations. In not-explicitly feminist social movements, participants and leaders ignore feminism at their peril. When participants in new mass movements choose to dam up feminist activism, they may motivate feminist separatism instead of forming coalitions with fierce, capable activists. The intersectional imperative provides a framework for future social movements to create larger, more sustainable coalitions of progressive feminist movements to amplify mass activism.

An Intersectional Revolution in Social Movements

Scholars Paula England (2010) and Kathleen Gerson (2010) describe American society's progress toward gender equality as a "stalled," "uneven," and "unfinished" gender revolution. Scholars of gender and organizations have revealed not only changes in cultural beliefs toward gender equality and the greater inclusion of women in the workplace but also the persistence of traditional gender stereotypes and continued reliance on men's leadership in contemporary workplace contexts and the family (Charles and Bradley 2002, 2009; Correll 2004; England 2010; Gerson 2010; Pedulla and Thébaud 2015; Ridgeway 2011). The mix of progress toward gender egalitarianism alongside many practices that continue to re-create traditional male–dominated hierarchies signals the "unevenness" and "unfinished" nature of social change toward equality.

The disproportionately white male–dominated collective identities, media, culture, and leadership of the Occupy movement point to a need for not only a gender revolution but an intersectional revolution. My assessment of the Occupy movement suggests that many forms of egalitarianism within it were limited and contested. Sexist *and* feminist processes shaped the movement. Racism *and* racial justice organizing characterized many of the encampments. Discrimination based on sexuality *and* queer politics contributed to the complexity of the movement. Participants experienced many forms of discrimination, often a combination of gender, race, class, and sexual inequalities. Expressions of discrimination alongside limited intersectional praxis within the movement point to the profound resilience of identity-based inequalities *and* the hope for progressive feminist social change.

This intersectional and feminist analysis of the Occupy movement's culture and structure suggests unfinished revolutions against sexism, racism, discrimination based on sexuality, *and* socioeconomic class inequality. Although the movement was intended to be nonhierarchical and widely mobilize men, women, and genderqueer participants from many racial/ethnic, socioeconomic, and sexual identities, conflicts plagued the movement, which limited the diversity of its leadership and rank-and-file membership. Yet some of the courageous Americans in the streets with the Occupy movement and activists who came after Occupy, such as the participants in Black Lives Matter and the Women's March, have envisioned a prefigurative future society that works toward the intersectional imperative. Participants in an intersectional revolution will listen to people who are of different identities than their own. By learning about their particular grievances, individuals can understand interlaced structures of inequality and embrace common causes. In an intersectional revolution, participants weave together preexisting social movements to form lasting mass movements for progressive social change. Social movements must not only spark the continuation of the gender revolution but kick-start a mass intersectional revolution using the intersectional imperative as a moral compass.

Methodological Appendix

This book is based on field research conducted between June and December 2012 in the two Occupy "movement centers" (Morris 1986) in New York City and the San Francisco Bay Area, as well as at the first Occupy National Gathering (NatGat) in Philadelphia. In each location, I gathered movement documents, such as flyers and newspapers.[1] Based on participant observation, I wrote extensive field notes. In addition, I conducted seventy-three in-depth semistructured interviews with key informants and spoke informally with dozens of other participants. I also created an archive of electronic documents that included copies of websites and discussion forums that participants used to publicize events and meeting minutes. This study also draws on a follow-up study about the continuation and transformation of the Occupy movement conducted in 2016 that included additional ethnography in New York City and the San Francisco Bay Area and another thirty-seven interviews.

Ethnographic Participant Observation

This study includes an ethnography of each field site created through participant observation. In New York, San Francisco, and Philadelphia, I observed and participated in the main Occupy movement events. I also collected data on the activities of the most significant feminist, women's, lesbian, gay, queer, and people of color groups and events in each field site.

I spent fifteen days at multi-event, all-day encampments and an additional twenty-five partial days at citywide meetings, protests, and cultural events. In total, I spent 155 hours in the field (70.5 in New York City, 32 in San Francisco/ Oakland, and 52.5 at NatGat). I spoke with a minimum of three people per event and easily fifteen or more at the encampments. I attended daytime and evening protests. Just a few of the events I studied included the first national Feminist General Assembly (FemGA) at NatGat; the movement's one-year anniversary on September 17, 2012, in New York; canvassing with the Oakland Anti-Foreclosure group about housing insecurity; and demonstrations in front of Citibank, Goldman Sachs, and Bank of America branches. I recorded field notes daily about the meetings, events, and people as well as critical reflections about my own subject position as a white female researcher and former activist.

To learn about the movement from multiple perspectives (Duneier 1999), I continually met, observed, and protested with a range of different people. While participating in the protests and meetings, I jotted notes in small pads. Later each day, I fleshed out the jottings and typed out or dictated full field notes into voice-recognition software (Emerson, Fretz, and Shaw 2011). I paused and reflected on my jottings several times a day to consider which regions of the encampments, meetings, and demographic groups I had inadvertently missed; then I visited and observed those spaces and people. During marches, rallies, and acts of civil disobedience, I was open and outgoing. I joined local events, meetings, and actions with ten or fewer participants and also national days of action with thousands of protesters. When I realized that I had been observing key organizers, I spent more time observing the rank-and-file membership. I observed participants of varied gender, race, sexual, age, and class identities.

In the field, I drew on my experiences as a feminist, student, and activist to participate in Occupy. To build rapport with participants, I utilized the organizational and communication skills that I had developed as a graduate student and activist in feminist, women's, anti-war, anti-globalization, and student movements. For example, I worked in the Women Occupy office in San Francisco for two weeks. I called volunteers, took conference call minutes, and participated in protests. I also helped plan Women Occupy protests at the 2012 Republican and Democratic National Conventions, where Women Occupy protesters advocated for women's and reproductive health issues by dressing in giant vagina costumes. In advance of the demonstrations, I generated lists of media contacts and a calendar of events that helped protesters navigate the convention and gain media attention. My participation in the movement's tactics, meetings, and discussions allowed me to intimately research Occupy and contribute to social change.

Interviews

While the media tended to overlook women Occupy participants of a variety of racial and ethnic identities, I created this study to give voice to them. I conducted seventy-three in-depth, semistructured key informant interviews with speakers, group meeting facilitators, writers and bloggers, and active rank-and-file protesters. In the tradition of feminist research (Taylor 1996, 1998), I conducted the majority of the interviews with women of a variety of races/ethnicities and sexual minorities, although I also interviewed a few white men. My research design is modeled on Belinda Robnett's (1997) and Mary Fonow's (2003) studies, which each engaged primarily women key informants to comprehensively examine social movement, gender, and racial dynamics. I located interviewees by advertising the study on Occupy Oakland (OO), Women Occupy, and New York General Assembly email discussion lists, snowball sampling, and meeting participants during protests. A few personal contacts from the University of California, Santa Barbara (UC Santa Barbara), and feminist and anti-war movements suggested lists of key informants whom I contacted while in the field. Because NatGat drew participants from major occupations across the United States, I recruited interviewees there from the western, southern, and northeastern regions. I have not included specific city locations for these participants to preserve their confidentiality.

This study goes beyond earlier research by including "genderqueer"[2] and "female and genderqueer" participants and participants with a range of racial/ethnic identities, 30% of whom identify as "persons of color." Participants included Native American, Latinx, Asian, Puerto Rican, Asian American, South Asian, Southeast Asian, Mexican/Aztec, Jewish, black, and mixed-race people (see Table A.1 for detailed demographic information). Among the interviewees, 80% identified as female, 7% identified as genderqueer, 7% identified as male, and 6% declined to answer. Approximately 60% of interviewees were white, and 40% identified as black, Asian, Latinx/Chicanx, or other race or declined to answer. With respect to sexuality, 42% of participants identified as heterosexual; 19% identified as gay, lesbian, or bisexual; 25% identified as queer or other sexuality; and 14% declined to answer. The interviewees ranged in age from eighteen to seventy-seven years old. Forty-seven interviewees indicated that they had stayed overnight in an Occupy encampment at some point during the first year of the movement. In terms of age, student status, non-Hispanic white identity, and education, interviewees in this study were similar to a representative sample of Occupy participants (see Table A.2 for a comparison).

The interviews were fun and often filled with laughter as key informants recalled exhilarating experiences. Interviews lasted from forty-five minutes to four hours (averaging about two hours) and followed an interview guide. We began by discussing how the interviewees came to participate in Occupy and how they contributed to working groups and protests. A few of the thirty questions I asked included the following: How are decisions made in Occupy? Who has the power to determine movement strategy and actions? Are there ways that participants in the movement strive to be inclusive? Through the flow of conversation, we discussed the movement's goals, strategies, organization, diversity, leadership, and collective identity. Many of the interviewees reported that Occupy protests had changed their lives. We spoke about actions and groups in which the participants felt particularly included or excluded, inequalities that

TABLE A.1 Interviewee Demographic Data

	New York City	San Francisco/ Oakland	Northeast	West	South	Total N
All Interviewees	28	21	11	9	4	73
Female	25	16	8	9	4	62
Male	2	2	2			6
"Genderqueer" or "Female and Genderqueer"	1	3	1			5
Age 18-24	6	3	2	2		13
Age 25-29	9	6		1	1	17
Age 30-39	8	6	1	1	2	18
Age 40-59	2	4	5	3	1	15
Age 60+	3	1		1		5
Age no response		1	3	1		5
Income $30K or less	13	10	6	3	3	35
Income $31-65K	9	3	1	1	1	15
Income $66+	2	1				3
Annual income no response	4	7	4	5		20
High school or less	1			2		3
Some college or BA	14	10	7	5	2	38
Graduate degree	11	10	4	1	2	28
Education no response	2	1		1		4
Currently a Student	5	6	4	2		17
*Black (2); Native American (1)	1	1			1	3
*Puerto Rican (2); Latinx (1); Chicanx (5)	5	2		1		8
*Asian American (3); South Asian (1)	2	2				4
*Mixed Race: Unspecified (1); White/Black (1); White/Latinx (1); White/Asian (1); White/ Southeast Asian (1); Mexican/ Aztec (1)	2	1	1	2		6
White (42) or "White and Jewish" (5)	17	15	7	5	3	47
Race No Response	1		3	1		5
Identify as "Person of Color"	9	7	2	2	2	22

*Aggregated to protect confidentiality.

TABLE A.2 Interviewee Characteristics Compared to Those of a
Representative OWS Sample

	Percent of total interviewees (n = 73) this study	Percent of total survey respondents (n = 727) from Milkman et al. (2013, 47)
Under 30 years old	41.1	37.1
Student	23.3	20.8
Non-Hispanic white	64.4	62.2
High school or less	4.1	7.9
Some college or bachelor's degree	52.0	47.4
Graduate degree	38.3	40.7

the interviewees experienced or observed in Occupy, and their prior involvement in feminist and other social movement organizations. The interviews examined infighting, tensions, and conflicts. Because the study reveals a variety of conflicts within contemporary activism, interviewees selected pseudonyms that I have used throughout the book to ensure confidentiality. Interviewees noted that movement-wide, Occupiers were reflecting on its achievements and strategies for future actions. The process of reflecting on the tactics and strategies of the movement during the interview became part of the action component of the research (Taylor 1998). We worked together to clarify the movement's strategies and actions through our discussions.

I transcribed all the interviews except for seven that were completed by an undergraduate research assistant. Using Dragon Naturally Speaking voice-recognition software, I transcribed the interviews word for word. I dictated each interview by listening to and speaking aloud the words that the interviewee had spoken. The transcription process mirrored an Occupy "mic check," a cultural ritual and protest tactic used by its participants. During a mic check, each individual spoke in short phrases, and the surrounding crowd repeated the speech phrase by phrase as a call-and-response chant (Kim 2011). Participants used mic checks to amplify the individual's speech without electronic sound systems. By repeating word for word the interviews to transcribe them, I mic checked them. As I transcribed, I removed identifying information.

The process was intimate and personal. I often laughed out loud or was brought to tears by repeating the heartfelt words and thoughts the interviewees had shared with me to create the voice recognition–generated transcript. Most interviewees explained that inequalities in the movement were infuriating but that the Occupy movement and feminism had changed their lives. Many described how they had found self-worth or that they had fulfilled life goals by participating in the movement. Catherine's emotional and existential realization about the importance of activism in her life is a representative example: "Feminism has been a lifesaver to me. Occupy and feminist activism gave me strength. Feminism means having a close connection with other women. Now I know why I'm here—I'm supposed to be working and helping other people. If I don't help other people in my life, then I feel like it's worthless." Although she was frustrated and sad about the oppression of women, Catherine was determined to change the world and felt pride in being an activist. As I repeated Catherine's and other interviewees' deeply heartfelt statements about their lives, inequalities, and social change, I immersed myself in the interview data and wrote memos about key ideas, themes, and methodological notes.

Archive of Documents and Websites

I assembled and analyzed an archive of paper and electronic documents and websites. The archive includes materials from Occupy Wall Street (OWS), OO, feminist spin-off groups, Women Occupy, and the feminist, queer, and people of color working groups in New York and the San Francisco Bay Area. At the encampments and from interviewees, I collected flyers, pamphlets, buttons, and signs.

The archive is an eclectic collection. From each organization's public website, I archived the main website, forum posts, the group's mission statement, conference-call transcripts, and meeting minutes. I archived articles about the movement from mainstream newspapers, such as the *New York Times* and the *San Francisco Chronicle*. Participants recorded most of the general assemblies at the encampments in the fall of 2011 in New York City and Oakland and posted the audio files online. I downloaded, saved, and listened to the general assembly audio recordings from each Occupy movement center. The archive includes "founding" documents from OWS that were read and referenced widely by the national movement, such as the "Declaration of the Occupation of New York City" and the movement's main newspapers, including *The Occupied Wall Street Journal*, *Occupy! An OWS-Inspired Gazette*, and *Tidal*. In the summer of 2012, to celebrate the one-year anniversary of Occupy, The Governors Galleries on Governors Island in New York City and the Yerba Buena Center for the Arts in San Francisco hosted exhibits of art, photographs, and posters from the Occupy movement. To archive these artifacts from the movement, I took digital photographs of each show. Images from the exhibits include a poster with the slogan "Occupy Sisterhood," a photograph of a female protester standing with a broom amid signs and tents at OWS, and images of women wearing tutus like the female dancer on top of *Charging Bull* who symbolized the Occupy movement prevailing over the financial industry.

The archive also includes documentation about feminist organizations and feminist collective actions within Occupy. From each feminist spin-off group and organization's public website, I archived the website content, public discussion forum, and mission statement. I also archived the documents that feminists used to create and plan the Feminist General Assemblies (FemGAs), such as conference-call minutes and discussion forums that were publicly available. I collected digital copies of the minutes and forums in addition to digital and paper flyers advertising the FemGAs. As with the citywide general assembly audio recordings, participants posted video and/or audio recordings from each FemGA. Research assistants and I downloaded these audio and video recordings and photos. We examined articles from feminist reporters, bloggers, and *Ms.* magazine to supplement the documents from feminist events and organizations in the archive.

This archive of documents enhanced my analysis of the field notes and interviews. Occupiers' conversations on discussion forums corroborated the interviewees' reports of protest events, conflicts, and the substance of discussions within and about the movement. Flyers about specific protest events and mission statements from spin-off organizations complemented interviewees' descriptions of protests, goals, and collective identities. By studying the movement's newspapers and articles from feminist magazines and bloggers, I traced the written history of intersectional conflicts in Occupy and the development of feminist mobilization. While the interviewees provided a wealth of context and explanation about protest events, the discussion forums included a wider and more comprehensive chronology of the calls for protest actions from the movement and the spin-off groups. In sum, I did not take my observations in the field or interviewees' stories "at face value" (Duneier 1999). To supplement and corroborate the ethnography and interviews, I triangulated the field notes and interviewees' stories with movement documents, online discussions among participants, and news reports from participants and journalists.

The Analysis

I generated the analysis by reflecting critically on thousands of observations. I immersed myself in the field notes and interviews by reading the transcripts multiple times. Using the mic-check transcription process, I became deeply familiar with each interview. I analyzed the paper archive by reading through the documents multiple times and broadly coding the contents into large thematic categories. For example, a research assistant and I grouped materials about feminism and gender together and created another category for materials about banking activism. As I read the field notes, interviews, and archives, I wrote memos about key themes (Groenewald 2008). Later, I used these memos to develop broad categories or "codes." These codes became the basis for analyzing the field notes, interviews, and archive with ATLAS.ti software. ATLAS.ti allowed me to code the qualitative data by categorizing text into broad themes and additional subthemes as needed. I wrote the analysis by editing and adding to the memos, summarizing reports from the ATLAS.ti coding, and referencing the paper archive.

Of course, social movements are not homogenous. By focusing on the movement's centers and NatGat, which served as Occupy's radical flanks, I may have underestimated the experiences of more moderate participants and organizations. In addition, I have not addressed the literally hundreds of local protests, the global dimensions of the movement (Calhoun 2013), the specific experiences of people with a range of identities such as people with disabilities and students, or anarchism (Bray 2013; Schneider 2013) and labor-union mobilization (Lewis and Luce 2012) that also contributed to nationwide action.

Feminist Methods for Studying Contemporary Activism

I drew on my insider, outsider, and "outsider-within[3] identities to analyze the movement. As an Occupier, researcher, and feminist activist, I participated in the research as an activist *and* scholar similar to other scholars of social movements (see, for example, Taylor 1998; Taylor and Rupp 2005). Throughout the study, I reflexively and critically examined these subject positions. Utilizing insider, outsider, and outsider-within perspectives, I grounded the analysis in a critical standpoint (P. Collins 1986; Haraway 1988). I reflected critically on my own attitudes and experiences about inequalities, women's participation in social movements, feminism, and my own subject position. At the same time, I completed the research using a feminist epistemology that views women's own meaning making as valid (Harding 1987). I encouraged the interviewees to define the trajectory of their stories and what was most important to their participation in the movement. While coding, I paid attention to the content and the linkages that participants made between concepts to inductively approach the data and ground it in each interviewee's explanations (D. Smith 2005; Sprague 2005). The analysis was driven by the narrative as defined by the interviewees, not the interviewer, to preserve the authenticity of the participants' experiences and their everyday lives (Reissman 1993; Sprague 2005).

Using feminist methodology, data, and analysis, this research creates feminist social change. As a participant observer, I attended and contributed to the first national Occupy FemGA. A few days later, with Women Occupy, we "Occupied the 4th of July." We stood in an act of civil disobedience, wearing signs that spelled out "Revolution Now" to disrupt the reading of the Declaration of Independence in Philadelphia. As part of the anniversary of Occupy in September 2012 in New York City, I joined the FemForce affinity group to help form a roving "wall" around Wall Street, and I forwarded group text messages for FemForce throughout the day. The roving "wall" protest propelled Occupy into a second year of mobilizations. By creating feminist social change, this research has empowered the researcher and participants.

Another objective of feminist research is to create relationships that endure beyond the data collection by "staying in the field" (Rupp and Taylor 2011). As I was wrapping up the interviews in December 2012, Hurricane Sandy ravaged the New York City area. Like many Occupy participants who shifted their activism to disaster relief, I joined Occupy Sandy in solidarity. I volunteered at Occupy Sandy disaster-relief distribution centers and sorted and distributed food and toiletries to the community. Occupy Sandy won praise and solidarity for the movement, because its members coordinated disaster relief more efficiently and comprehensively than even the Red Cross (see, for example, Feuer 2012). I participated in Occupy events in Santa Barbara and New York through 2016. I helped organize a movement-building event for Occupiers, feminists, and peace activists in Santa Barbara; I hosted in my home Occupy activists who were traveling across the country to organize; and I contributed to several Alternative Banking Working Group events in New York City. I also joined former Occupy participants and student-of-color organizations at UC Santa Barbara to organize an anti-racism and gun-control teach-in to memorialize Trayvon Martin and protest his death. By participating in spin-off protests with other Occupiers and feminists, I continued to "go back and give back" (Rupp and Taylor 2011).

Feminist research is participatory action research that transforms public opinion about gender inequality. Through a series of presentations about this research, I spoke out about intersectional conflicts in Occupy and mobilization to create inclusivity. Just a few of the ways in which I have spread the knowledge gained from this study to the public include dozens of presentations at universities, community groups, national and international scholarly conferences, and a two-hour special radio show on KCSB radio, based in Santa Barbara. Audience members included sociologists, feminists, faculty and students, activists, and the public. Comments and questions from the audiences helped me clarify the data analysis.

Throughout the research process, I have collected and analyzed qualitative data to produce a subjective and critical study of the Occupy movement. The data have contributed to a partial analysis of the movement, which prioritizes the voices of Occupiers, women, and queer people of a variety of racial/ethnic and sexual identities. Because the research includes NatGat participants and representatives from the most nationally influential city-based encampments in New York City and the San Francisco Bay Area, the study contributes to understanding the national movement.

Notes

Introduction

1. Divulging gender pronouns is a cultural practice in alliance with transgender rights, feminist, and lesbian, gay, bisexual, transgender, and queer/questioning (LGBTQ) movements. Each individual shares the pronoun that appropriately refers to his/her/their gender identity. The practice recognizes that gender is a socially constructed process (West and Zimmerman 1987). By sharing gender pronouns, individuals can reveal their gender identities, which may or may not correspond to their performance of femininity or masculinity. In addition, individuals who are gender nonconforming, transgender individuals who eschew identifying as either male or female, and any other individual who chooses de-gendered language and cultural practices (Manjoo 2019) can signal their gender pronoun as "they" or a range of other nongendered pronouns.

2. "Intersectionality" is the analytical practice to examine how gender, race, class, and other inequalities are intertwined. Many individuals experience multiple inequalities and an escalation of those inequalities by being at the "intersection." Kimberlé Crenshaw (1989) coined the term to encapsulate the experience of black women who endure not only racism or sexism but particular disadvantages by living at the intersection of racial and gender inequalities. The concept is explained in greater detail later in this chapter.

3. "Flash mobs" are cultural practices that can be used as a social movement tactic. Usually, individuals are called to action over social media, text

messaging, email, or blogging. The call instructs individuals to gather in a particular place at a particular time. Seemingly spontaneously, the group of individuals engages in a coordinated theater, dance, or music activity that is unique for that particular space. Typically, participants engage in flash mobs to provide humor and entertainment, call attention to a collective grievance, raise awareness, or achieve a combination of these goals. Flash mobs usually involve between ten and one hundred people. For example, pilots and flight attendants might engage in a choreographed dance to a pop song in the middle of an airport to entertain weary travelers.

4. #SayHerName began as a report about police brutality against black women in the United States, researched and written by the African American Policy Forum; the Center for Intersectionality and Social Policy Studies at Columbia Law School; Andrea Ritchie, Soros Justice Fellow; and experts on the policing of women and LGBTQ people of color. Led by Columbia Law School professor Kimberlé Crenshaw, the hashtag became widespread. As Crenshaw and others popularized the hashtag, individuals and grassroots groups created street and online demonstrations to continue to expose and protest violence against black women. For more information, see http://aapf.org/sayhernamereport.

5. "Big-tent" mass movements aim to include a wide range of participants. Participants may have diverse personal identities or political beliefs.

6. The dissertation, published in 2015, focuses on the following questions: How do masculinity, femininity, and genderqueer processes influence contemporary mixed-sex social movement dynamics and culture? What role did feminist identity, tactics, and leadership play in the emergence and development of Occupy? How did feminist mobilizing structures outside Occupy contribute to the movement?

7. I have adapted the term "outsider-within" that Patricia Hill Collins (1986) originally coined to refer to the experiences of black women in academia. Here I have modified the term to encapsulate the experience of feminists who are marginalized within other social movements.

8. The "sociological imagination" is a term coined by C. Wright Mills (1959). Sociological imagination is the analytical process of connecting one's personal experiences and troubles to larger public issues and structural arrangements that shape social problems. The analytical process guides researchers to create relevant and impactful sociological studies that are grounded in individuals' lived experiences.

9. "Free spaces" are gatherings within social movements that are not controlled by the overall movement's leadership. In free spaces, individuals and groups take time to develop social-change initiatives that the larger movement's leaders might view as unique, too risky, or beyond the status quo. Free spaces often yield innovations for creating social change. For more on free spaces, see Allen 1970 and Polletta and Kretschmer 2013.

Chapter 1

1. At the time of interviews in 2012, participants specified their identities as Chicana and not Xicana or Xicanx. In the 2010s, some persons have decided to use the terms Xicana, Xicano, or Xicanx rather than Chicana, Chicano, or Chicanx to embrace spelling conventions common in the indigenous Nahuatl language and to recognize their indigenous ancestry (Moraga 2011).

2. Posted on December 3, 2011, by Morning Star Gali on the Occupy Oakland discussion blog (https://occupyoakland.org/2011/12/decolonize-oakland/).

3. Occupy the Hood indicates Occupy the "neighborhood." Hood is a slang term that refers to inner city areas in the United States populated by black persons.

4. CODEPINK is a grassroots women-led peace and human-rights organization that was founded in the United States in 2002. At the time of publication, CODEPINK has grown into a worldwide network.

5. "LGBTIQA2Z" stands for the Lesbian Gay Bisexual Transgender Intersex Queer or Questioning Asexual or Allies Two-Spirited Zhe Zher Gender Neutral Pronouns Caucus.

6. Typically, "trannies" is a derogatory term for transvestites. In this case, activists are proud to reclaim the label and celebrate their queer identity.

7. Sylvia Rivera was a drag queen and leader of gay liberation and transgender rights movements in New York City in the 1960s and 1970s.

Chapter 2

1. "Working groups" was the Occupy movement's name for committees.

2. See http://hotchicksofoccupywallstreet.tumblr.com/ (accessed on April 4, 2018).

3. "Mactivists" is a term of derision that was used by feminist activists in Oakland and other locations in 2012 and possibly at other times in the contemporary era in the United States. Mactivists attend social movement gatherings with the intention to date or harass other activists. The label refers especially to men who make sexual advances toward women.

4. Information about the cards can be found at http://www.52shadesofgreed .com (accessed on July 6, 2015).

5. The publication is available at http://strikedebt.org/The-Debt-Resistors -Operations-Manual.pdf (accessed on September 3, 2019).

6. The Anonymous movement was developed by a decentralized group of "hactivists," or activists who create websites and use internet-based tools to disrupt organizations and practices that they perceive as unjust.

7. The practice of using Preferred Gender Pronouns (PGPs) allowed individuals to choose the pronoun that best fit their gender presentation. However, the tactic changed shortly after the Occupy movement to be described only as a process of sharing one's "gender pronouns." Activists removed the "preferred"

adjective to acknowledge that the pronouns that cisgender, transgender, and genderqueer participants use are not just a preference or opinion but their actual pronouns.

Chapter 3

1. Bennett J. Tepper, Michelle Duffy, and Jason Shaw (2001) argue that follower input may either impede leaders' work ("dysfunctional resistance") or provide an opportunity for leaders to change their leadership strategies ("constructive resistance"). In this chapter, I present examples of an additional form of follower resistance: "discriminatory resistance." Followers who impede leaders by acting implicitly or explicitly on racial and gendered prejudices perform discriminatory resistance.

2. The "leadership labyrinth" concept was developed by Alice Eagly and Linda Carli (2007).

3. To protect confidentiality, the specific mixed-racial background is not revealed.

4. To protect confidentiality, the specific mixed-racial background is not revealed.

Chapter 4

1. Other topics featured in the journal include transgender rights organizing; the 2006 popular uprising in Oaxaca, Mexico; police repression; debates about sexuality; Communism; and other mass revolutionary movements.

2. The quote appears in Vol. 1, 2012 (Creative Commons Attribution—Noncommercial License), available at http://www.liesjournal.net/. "Materialist feminism" is a philosophy that brings together the ideas of Marxism and feminism. Materialist feminists analyze women's economic oppressions as being based on class *and* gender inequalities.

3. Kickstarter is a website (https://www.kickstarter.com/) where individuals and groups can raise funds for creative goals, such as books, music recordings, board games, videos, small businesses, and other self-published or entrepreneurial projects.

4. "Gender conflict" is an umbrella term for conflicts that disadvantage, threaten, or harm women, genderqueer persons, and sexual minorities. Gender conflicts are a form of contention over issues pertaining to gender inequality and inhibit the development of intersectional praxis. They develop primarily in response to gender inequality when subordinated groups, including women, trans persons, and sexual minorities, challenge male domination and vocalize the exclusion and oppressions they face in social movements.

5. "LGBTIQA2Z" stands for the Lesbian Gay Bisexual Transgender Intersex Queer or Questioning Asexual or Allies Two-Spirited Zhe Zher Gender Neutral Pronouns Caucus.

6. See the entry at https://oaklandoccupypatriarchy.wordpress.com/points -of-unity (accessed on September 3, 2019).

7. The use of quotation marks in the phrase feminist "free spaces" indicates that these were locations and contexts within the Occupy movement where feminists controlled the culture, politics, and other movement dynamics. The quotation marks emphasize that these were not spaces absent of feminist activity; on the contrary, these were explicitly feminist contexts separate from the main movement where feminists could take on the majority of speaking, leading, strategizing, and other decisions.

Conclusion

1. The Guy Fawkes mask depicts a masculine white face with black facial hair. It became a symbol of the Anonymous movement and the Occupy movement.

2. Although data about Bernie Sanders's 2020 presidential campaign were not a part of this research study, future research should examine whether and how these same Facebook networks that developed during the Occupy movement and the 2016 presidential campaign were again in use in 2019 and 2020.

3. "Black Twitter" refers to an online network of people who dialogue about and develop a community of black persons and black culture online. Using Twitter, a micro-blogging platform, bloggers, public intellectuals, citizen journalists, and other black people exchange views about especially black culture and racial justice.

4. For more about Black Lives Matter, the Movement for Black Lives, and their intersectional analysis and praxis, see https://policy.m4bl.org/platform/ (accessed on September 3, 2019).

Methodological Appendix

1. Hundreds of the archival documents have been digitized and are available publicly in the Occupy Archive at https://doi.org/10.17605/OSF.IO/6V9ZF.

2. "Genderqueer" and "female and genderqueer" persons identify not as men or women but as another gender identity. Genderqueer is an umbrella term for persons who do not conform to the gender binary. Genderqueer persons may present themselves using unique gendered expressions or conforming to traditional expressions of masculinity, femininity, and/or androgyny.

3. I have adapted the term "outsider-within" that Patricia Hill Collins (1986) originally coined to refer to the experiences of black women in academia. Here I have modified the term to encapsulate the experience of feminists who are marginalized within other social movements.

References

Abileah, Rae. 2012. "Why I Broke Up with Bank of America." *Pink Tank*, February 22. Accessed September 18, 2019. Available at https://www.codepink.org /why_i_broke_up_with_bank_of_america.

Allen, Chude Pamela. 1970. *Free Space: A Perspective on the Small Group in Women's Liberation*. New York: *Times Change Press*.

Anzaldúa, Gloria. 1987. *Borderlands: La Frontera*. San Francisco: Aunt Lute Books.

Arat, Yeşim. 2019. "Feminist Movement and the Women of the Gezi Park Protests." Paper presented at European Conference on Politics and Gender, July 6, Amsterdam, Netherlands.

Baker, Al, Colin Moyinihan, and Sarah Maslin Nir. 2011. "Police Arrest More Than 700 Protesters on Brooklyn Bridge." *New York Times*, October 1. Accessed December 15, 2014. Available at http://cityroom.blogs.nytimes.com /2011/10/01/police-arresting-protesters-on-brooklyn-bridge/?_r=0.

Barker, Adam J. 2012. "Already Occupied: Indigenous Peoples, Settler Colonialism and the Occupy Movements in North America." *Social Movement Studies* 11 (3–4): 327–334.

Bates, Karen Grigsby. 2018. "A Look Back at Trayvon Martin's Death, and the Movement It Inspired." *National Public Radio*, July 31. Accessed September 18, 2019. Available at https://www.npr.org/sections/codeswitch/2018/07/31 /631897758/a-look-back-at-trayvon-martins-death-and-the-movement-it -inspired.

Beckwith, Karen. 1996. "Lancashire Women against Pit Closures: Women's Standing in a Men's Movement." *Signs: Journal of Women in Culture and Society* 21 (4): 1034–1068.

Beeman, Angie. 2015. "Walk the Walk but Don't Talk the Talk: The Strategic Use of Color-Blind Ideology in an Interracial Social Movement Organization." *Sociological Forum* 30 (1): 127–147.

Benford, Robert D., and David A. Snow. 2000. "Framing Processes and Social Movements: An Overview and Assessment." *Annual Review of Sociology* 26 (1): 611–639.

Bernstein, Mary. 2008. "The Analytical Dimensions of Identity: A Political Identity Framework." In *Identity Work in Social Movements*, edited by Jo Reger, Daniel J. Myers, and Rachel Einwohner, 277–297. Minneapolis: University of Minnesota Press.

Bernstein, Mary, and Verta Taylor, eds. 2013. *The Marrying Kind? Debating Same-Sex Marriage within the Lesbian and Gay Movement*. Minneapolis: University of Minnesota Press.

Blee, Kathleen M. 2002. *Inside Organized Racism: Women in the Hate Movement*. Berkeley: University of California Press.

———. 2012. *Democracy in the Making: How Activist Groups Form*. Oxford: Oxford University Press.

Blee, Kathleen M., and Verta Taylor. 2002. "Semi-structured Interviewing in Social Movement Research." In *Methods in Social Movement Research*, edited by Bert Klandermans and Suzanne Staggenborg, 92–117. Minneapolis: University of Minnesota Press.

Bonilla-Silva, Eduardo. 2006. *Racism without Racists: Color-Blind Racism and the Persistence of Racial Inequality in the United States*. Lanham, MD: Rowman & Littlefield.

Boothroyd, Sydney, Rachelle Bowen, Alicia Cattermole, Kenda Chang-Swanson, Hanna Daltrop, Sasha Dwyer, Anna Gunn, Brydon Kramer, Delaney M. McCartan, Jasmine Nagra, Shereen Samimi, and Qwisun Yoon-Potkins, 2017. "(Re)producing Feminine Bodies: Emergent Spaces through Contestation in the Women's March on Washington." *Gender, Place & Culture* 24 (5): 711–721.

Bray, Marc. 2013. *Translating Anarchy: The Anarchism of Occupy Wall Street*. London: Zero Books.

Breines, Wini. 1989. *Community and Organization in the New Left, 1962–1968: The Great Refusal*. New Brunswick, NJ: Rutgers University Press.

Brescoll, Victoria L. 2016. "Leading with Their Hearts? How Gender Stereotypes of Emotion Lead to Biased Evaluations of Female Leaders." *Leadership Quarterly* 27 (3): 415–428.

Bridges, Tristan S. 2010. "Men Just Weren't Made to Do This: Performances of Drag at 'Walk a Mile in Her Shoes' Marches." *Gender & Society* 24 (1): 5–30.

Brown, Melissa, Rashawn Ray, Ed Summers, and Neil Fraistat. 2017. "#SayHer-Name: A Case Study of Intersectional Social Media Activism." *Ethnic and Racial Studies* 40 (11): 1831–1846.

Brunner, Mikki. 2011. "Who Are the Black Women Occupying Wall Street?" In *The 99%: How the Occupy Wall Street Movement Is Changing America*, edited by Lynn Parramore, Tara Lohan, and Don Hazen, 76–77. San Francisco: AlterNet.

Bulwa, Demian, and Rachel Swan. 2018. "10 Years Since Oscar Grant's Death: What Happened at Fruitvale Station?" *SFChronicle.com*, December 28. Accessed September 18, 2019. Available at https://www.sfchronicle.com/bayarea/article/10-years-since-Oscar-Grant-s-death-What-13489585.php.

Butler, Judith. 2012. "So What Are the Demands? And Where Do They Go from Here?" *Tidal: Occupy Theory, Occupy Strategy* 1 (2): 8–11.

Butler, Melanie. 2011. "Finding Our Voices and Creating Safe Spaces at Occupy Wall Street." In *The 99%: How the Occupy Wall Street Movement Is Changing America*, edited by Lynn Parramore, Tara Lohan, and Don Hazen, 71–73. San Francisco: AlterNet.

Cagle, Susie. 2011. "The Hand Signals of the Occupation." In *The 99%: How the Occupy Wall Street Movement Is Changing America*, edited by Lynn Parramore, Tara Lohan, and Don Hazen, 59. San Francisco: AlterNet.

Calhoun, Craig. 2013. "Occupy Wall Street in Perspective." *British Journal of Sociology* 64 (1): 26–38.

Campbell, Emahunn Raheem Ali. 2011. "A Critique of the Occupy Movement from a Black Occupier." *Black Scholar* 41 (4): 42–51.

Carastathis, Anna. 2013. "Identity Categories as Potential Coalitions." *Signs: Journal of Women in Culture and Society* 38 (4): 941–965.

———. 2016. *Intersectionality: Origins, Contestations, Horizons*. Lincoln: University of Nebraska Press.

Charles, Maria, and Karen Bradley. 2002. "Equal but Separate? A Cross-national Study of Sex Segregation in Higher Education." *American Sociological Review* 67 (4): 573–599.

———. 2009. "Indulging Our Gendered Selves? Sex Segregation by Field of Study in 44 Countries." *American Journal of Sociology* 114 (4): 924–976.

Cho, Sumi, Kimberlé Williams Crenshaw, and Leslie McCall. 2013. "Toward a Field of Intersectionality Studies: Theory, Applications, and Praxis." *Signs: Journal of Women in Culture and Society* 38 (4): 785–810.

Choo, Hae Yeon, and Myra Marx Ferree. 2010. "Practicing Intersectionality in Sociological Research: A Critical Analysis of Inclusions, Interactions, and Institutions in the Study of Inequalities." *Sociological theory* 28 (2): 129–149.

Chun, Jennifer Jihye, George Lipsitz, and Young Shin. 2013. "Intersectionality as a Social Movement Strategy: Asian Immigrant Women Advocates." *Signs: Journal of Women in Culture and Society* 38 (4): 917–940.

Cohen, Noam. 2008. "Sisters in Idiosyncrasy." *New York Times,* March 30. Accessed November 18, 2014. Available at http://www.nytimes.com/2008/03 /30/fashion/30sanfrooklyn.html?pagewanted=all.

Collins, Patricia Hill. 1986. "Learning from the Outsider Within: The Sociological Significance of Black Feminist Thought." *Social Problems* 33 (6): S14–S32.

Collins, Patricia Hill, and Sirma Bilge. 2016. *Intersectionality.* Hoboken, NJ: John Wiley & Sons.

Collins, Terry. 2011. "Scott Olsen, Iraq War Veteran, Injured by Police during 'Occupy Oakland' Protest." *Huffington Post,* October 26. Accessed November 19, 2014. Available at http://www.huffingtonpost.com/2011/10/26/scott -olsen-iraq-war-veteran-injured_n_1034003.html.

Connell, Raewyn W. 2005. *Masculinities.* Cambridge, UK: Polity.

Connell, Raewyn W., and James W. Messerschmidt. 2005. "Hegemonic Masculinity: Rethinking the Concept." *Gender & Society* 19 (6): 829–859.

Correll, Shelly J. 2004. "Constraints into Preferences: Gender, Status, and Emerging Career Aspirations." *American Sociological Review* 69 (1): 93–113.

Crenshaw, Kimberlé Williams. 1989. "Demarginalizing the Intersection of Race and Sex: A Black Feminist Critique of Antidiscrimination Doctrine, Feminist Theory and Antiracist Politics." *University of Chicago Legal Forum* 1989 (1): 139–167.

Crossley, Alison Dahl. 2017. *Finding Feminism: Millennial Activists and the Unfinished Gender Revolution.* New York: New York University Press.

Debt Resistors. 2012. *Debt Resistors' Operation Manual.* Accessed June 18, 2018. Available at http://strikedebt.org/The-Debt-Resistors-Operations-Manual .pdf.

DeRue, D. Scott, and Susan J. Ashford. 2010. "Who Will Lead and Who Will Follow? A Social Process of Leadership Identity Construction in Organizations." *Academy of Management Review* 35 (4): 627–647.

Diehl, Amy B., and Leanne Dzubinski. 2017. "An Overview of Gender-Based Leadership Barriers." In *Handbook of Research on Gender and Leadership,* edited by Susan Madsen, 271–286. Cheltenham, UK: Edward Elgar.

Duneier, Mitchell. 1999. *Sidewalk.* New York: Frarrar, Straus, and Giroux.

Eagly, Alice Hendrickson, and Linda Lorene Carli. 2007. *Through the Labyrinth: The Truth about How Women Become Leaders.* Boston: Harvard Business Press.

Emerson, Robert M., Rachel I. Fretz, and Linda L. Shaw. 2011. *Writing Ethnographic Fieldnotes.* Chicago: University of Chicago Press.

England, Paula. 2010. "The Gender Revolution: Uneven and Stalled." *Gender & Society* 24 (2): 149–166.

Eschle, Catherine. 2016. "Troubling Stories of the End of Occupy: Feminist Narratives of Betrayal at Occupy Glasgow." *Social Movement Studies* 17 (5): 524–540.

Espiritu, Yến Lê. 2008. *Asian American Women and Men: Labor, Laws, and Love.* Lanham, MD: Rowman and Littlefield.

Evans, Sara. 1979. *Personal Politics: The Roots of Women's Liberation in the Civil Rights Movement*. New York: Vintage.

Faludi, Susan. 2006. *Backlash: The Undeclared War against American Women*. New York: Broadway Books.

Ferree, Myra Marx. 2009. "Inequality, Intersectionality and the Politics of Discourse: Framing Feminist Alliances." In *The Discursive Politics of Gender Equality: Stretching, Bending and Policymaking*, edited by Emanuela Lombardo, Petra Meier, and Mieke Verloo, 84–101. Abingdon-on-Thames, UK: Routledge/ECPR Studies in European Political Science.

Feuer, Alan. 2012. "Occupy Sandy: A Movement Moves to Relief." *New York Times,* November 9. Accessed November 19, 2014. Available at http://www.nytimes.com/2012/11/11/nyregion/where-fema-fell-short-occupy-sandy-was-there.html?pagewanted=all.

Fisher, Melissa. 2012. *Wall Street Women*. Durham, NC: Duke University Press.

Fonow, Mary Margaret. 2003. *Union Women: Forging Feminism in the United Steelworkers of America*. Minneapolis: Minnesota University Press.

Freedman, Estelle. 1995. "Separatism as Strategy: Female Institution Building and American Feminism 1870–1930." In *Feminism and Community*, edited by Penny A. Weiss and Marilyn Friedman, 85–104. Philadelphia: Temple University Press.

Freeman, Jo. 1975. *The Politics of Women's Liberation: A Case Study of an Emerging Social Movement and Its Relation to the Policy Process*. New York: Longman.

Gaby, Sarah, and Neal Caren. 2016. "The Rise of Inequality: How Social Movements Shape Discursive Fields." *Mobilization: An International Quarterly* 21 (4): 413–429.

Gamson, Joshua. 1997. "Messages of Exclusion: Gender, Movements, and Symbolic Boundaries." *Gender & Society* 11 (2): 178–199.

Gamson, William A. 1975. *The Strategy of Social Protest*. Homewood, IL: Dorsey Press.

Garza, Alicia. 2014. "A Herstory of the #BlackLivesMatter Movement." *Feminist Wire,* October 7. Accessed September 13, 2017. Available at http://www.thefeministwire.com/2014/10/blacklivesmatter-2/.

Gerson, Kathleen. 2010. *The Unfinished Revolution: How a New Generation Is Reshaping Family, Work, and Gender in America*. Oxford: Oxford University Press.

Ghaziani, Amin. 2008. *The Dividends of Dissent: How Conflict and Culture Work in Lesbian and Gay Marches on Washington*. Chicago: University of Chicago Press.

Giddens, Anthony. 1990. *The Consequences of Modernity*. Stanford, CA: Stanford University Press.

Gillham, Patrick F., Bob Edwards, and John A. Noakes. 2013. "Strategic Incapacitation and the Policing of Occupy Wall Street Protests in New York City, 2011." *Policing and Society* 23 (1): 81–102.

Gitlin, Todd. 2012. *Occupy Nation.* New York: Harper Collins.

Goffman, Erving. 1959. *The Presentation of Self in Everyday Life.* Garden City, NY: Doubleday Anchor Books.

Goss, Kristin A. 2017. "The Swells between the 'Waves': American Women's Activism, 1920–1965." In *The Oxford Handbook of U.S. Women's Social Movement Activism*, edited by Holly J. McCammon, Lee Ann Banaszak, Verta Taylor, and Jo Reger, 51–70. New York: Oxford University Press.

Gould-Wartofsky, Michael A. 2015. *The Occupiers: The Making of the 99 Percent Movement.* New York: Oxford University Press.

Graeber, David. 2011. "The Strange Success of Occupy Wall Street." In *The 99%: How the Occupy Wall Street Movement Is Changing America*, edited by Lynn Parramore, Tara Lohan, and Don Hazen, 25–29. San Francisco: AlterNet.

Groenewald, Thomas. 2008. "Memos and Memoing." In *The SAGE Encyclopedia of Qualitative Research Methods*, edited by Lisa M. Given, 505–506. Thousand Oaks, CA: SAGE.

Hafez, Sherine. 2014. "Bodies That Protest: The Girl in the Blue Bra, Sexuality, and State Violence in Revolutionary Egypt." *Signs: Journal of Women in Culture and Society* 40 (1): 20–28.

Halberstam, J. Jack. 2012. *Gaga Feminism: Sex, Gender, and the End of Normal.* Boston: Beacon Press.

Hammond, John. 2015. "The Anarchism of Occupy Wall Street." *Science and Society* 79 (2): 288–313.

Haraway, Donna. 1988. "Situated Knowledges: The Science Question in Feminism and the Privilege of Partial Perspective." *Feminist Studies* 14 (3): 575–599.

Hardikar, Ashwini. 2011. "The Value of a Safe Space: One WOC's Experience with Harassment at Occupy Wall Street." *In Front and Center: Critical Voices in the 99%*, October 13. Accessed October 1, 2019. Available at https://infrontandcenter.wordpress.com/2011/10/13/the-value-of-a-safe-space/.

Harding, Sandra G. 1987. *Feminism and Methodology.* Bloomington: Indiana University.

Hernandez, Jesus. 2009. "Redlining Revisited: Mortgage Lending Patterns in Sacramento 1930–2004." *International Journal of Urban and Regional Research* 33 (2): 291–313.

Hess, Amanda. 2016. "Everyone Is Wrong about the Bernie Bros: How a Necessary Critique of Leftist Sexism Deteriorated into a Dumb Flame War." *Slate*, February 3. Accessed September 16, 2019. Available at https://slate.com/technology/2016/02/bernie-bros-are-bad-the-conversation-around-them-is-worse.html.

Hoyt, Crystal L., and Susan E. Murphy. 2016. "Managing to Clear the Air: Stereotype Threat, Women, and Leadership." *Leadership Quarterly* 27 (3): 387–399.

Hunt, Scott A., and Robert D. Benford. 2004. "Collective Identity, Solidarity, and Commitment." In *The Blackwell Companion to Social Movements*, edited by David A. Snow, Sarah A. Soule, and Hans Kriesi, 433–458. Oxford: Blackwell.

Hurwitz, Heather McKee. 2017. "From Ink to Web and Beyond: U.S. Women's Activism Using Traditional and New Social Media." In *The Oxford Handbook of U.S. Women's Social Movement Activism*, edited by Holly J. McCammon, Lee Ann Banaszak, Verta Taylor, and Jo Reger, 462–483. New York: Oxford University Press.

———. 2019. "#FemGA #SayHerName #NotHereForBoys: Feminist Spillover in US Social Movements 2011–2016." In *Nevertheless They Persisted: Feminisms and Continued Resistance in the U.S. Women's Movement*, edited by Jo Reger, 115–132. Abingdon, UK: Routledge Press.

Hurwitz, Heather McKee, and Alison Dahl Crossley. 2019. "Gender and Social Movements." In *Wiley-Blackwell Companion to Social Movements*, 2nd ed., edited by David Snow, Sarah Soule, Hanspeter Kriesi, and Holly McCammon, 537–552. Oxford: Wiley-Blackwell.

Irvine, Jill, Sabine Lang, and Celeste Montoya, eds. 2019. *Gendered Mobilizations and Intersectional Challenges: Contemporary Social Movements in Europe and North America*. London: Rowman and Littlefield.

Jackman, Mary. 2006. "Gender, Violence, and Harassment." In *Handbook of the Sociology of Gender*, edited by Janet Saltzman Chafetz, 275–317. New York: Kluwer Academic/Plenum.

Jacobs, Katrien. 2016. "Disorderly Conduct: Feminist Nudity in Chinese Protest Movements." *Sexualities* 19 (7): 819–835.

Juris, Jeffrey S., Michelle Ronayne, Firuzeh Shokooh-Valle, and Robert Wengronowitz. 2012. "Negotiating Power and Difference within the 99%." *Social Movement Studies* 11 (3–4): 434–440.

Kim, Richard. 2011. "The Human Microphone." In *The 99%: How the Occupy Wall Street Movement Is Changing America*, edited by Lynn Parramore, Tara Lohan, and Don Hazen, 62–64. San Francisco: AlterNet.

King, Deborah H. 1988. "Multiple Jeopardy, Multiple Consciousness: The Context of a Black Feminist Ideology." *Signs: Journal of Women in Culture and Society* 14 (1): 42–72.

King, Mike. 2013. "Disruption Is Not Permitted: The Policing and Social Control of Occupy Oakland." *Critical Criminology* 21 (4): 463–475.

Kingkade, Tyler. 2011. "Occupy Cal Berkeley Protest Draws Thousands, as Two Years of Occupation Come Home." *Huffington Post*, November 11. Accessed November 19, 2014. Available at http://www.huffingtonpost.com/2011/11/10/thousands-gather-for-occupy-cal-protest_n_1086963.html.

Kramer, Vicki W., Alison M. Conrad, and Sumru Erkut. 2006. "Critical Mass on Corporate Boards: Why Three or More Women Enhance Governance." *Wellesley Centers for Women's Publications Office*. Accessed February 27, 2018. Available at https://www.wcwonline.org/pdf/CriticalMassExecSummary.pdf.

Laperrière, Marie, and Eléonore Lépinard. 2016. "Intersectionality as a Tool for Social Movements: Strategies of Inclusion and Representation in the Québécois Women's Movement." *Politics* 36 (4): 374–382.

Lépinard, Eléonore. 2007. "The Contentious Subject of Feminism: Defining *Women* in France from the Second Wave to Parity." *Signs: Journal of Women in Culture and Society* 32 (2): 375–403.

Leach, Darcy K. 2013. "Culture and the Structure of Tyrannylessness." *Sociological Quarterly* 54 (2): 181–191.

Lewis, Peggy, and Luce, Stephanie. 2012. "Labor and Occupy Wall Street: An Appraisal of the First Six Months." *New Labor Forum* 21 (2): 43–49.

Liboiron, Max. 2012. "Tactics of Waste, Dirt and Discard in the Occupy Movement." *Social Movement Studies* 11 (3–4): 393–401.

LIES Collective. 2012. LIES: *A Journal of Materialist Feminism*. Vol. 1. Accessed April 22, 2020. Available at https://www.liesjournal.net/lies-volume1.pdf.

Liu, Helena, Leanne Cutcher, and David Grant. 2015. "Doing Authenticity: The Gendered Construction of Authentic Leadership." *Gender, Work and Organization* 22 (3): 237–255.

Lomax, Tamura. 2011. "Occupy Rape Culture." *Feminist Wire*, November 5. Accessed September 28, 2019. Available at http://thefeministwire.com/2011/11/occupy-rape-culture/.

López, Marta Cruells, and Sonia Ruiz García. 2014. "Political Intersectionality within the Spanish Indignados Social Movement." In *Intersectionality and Social Change, Research in Social Movements, Conflicts and Change*, vol. 37, edited by Lynne M. Woehrle, 3–25. Bingley, UK: Emerald Group.

Lubin, Judy. 2012. "The 'Occupy' Movement: Emerging Protest Forms and Contested Urban Spaces." *Berkeley Planning Journal* 25 (1): 184–197.

Luft, Rachel E. 2016. "Racialized Disaster Patriarchy: An Intersectional Model for Understanding Disaster Ten Years after Hurricane Katrina." *Feminist Formations* 28 (2): 1–26.

Maharawal, Manissa. 2011. "Standing Up." In *Occupy! Scenes from Occupied America*, edited by Astra Taylor, Keith Gessen, and editors from *N+1, Dissent, Triple Canopy*, and the *New Inquiry*, 34–40. Brooklyn: Verso.

———. 2016. "Occupy Movements." In *Wiley Blackwell Encyclopedia of Gender and Sexuality Studies*, edited by Nancy Naples, 1–5. Oxford: Blackwell.

Mahler, Jonathan. 2012. "Oakland, the Last Refuge of Radical America." *New York Times*, August 1. Accessed August 5, 2011. Available at http://www.nytimes.com/2012/08/05/magazine/oakland-occupy-movement.html?pagewanted=all&_r=0.

Manilov, Marianne. 2013. "Occupy at One Year: Growing the Roots of a Movement." *Sociological Quarterly* 54 (2): 206–213.

Manjoo, Farhad. 2019. "Opinion: It's Time for 'They.'" *New York Times*, July 10. Accessed September 24, 2019. Available at https://www.nytimes.com/2019/07/10/opinion/pronoun-they-gender.html?module=inline.

McCammon, Holly J., Courtney Sanders Muse, Harmony D. Newman, and Teresa M. Terrell. 2007. "Movement Framing and Discursive Opportunity Structures: The Political Successes of the U.S. Women's Jury Movements." *American Sociological Review* 72 (5): 725–749.

McNight, Matthew. 2012. "The Meaning of the Trayvon Martin Case." *New Yorker*, July 10. Accessed September 21, 2019. Available at https://www.newyorker.com/news/news-desk/the-meaning-of-the-trayvon-martin-case.

McVeigh, Karen. 2011. "Occupy Wall Street's Women Struggle to Make Their Voices Heard." *Guardian*, November 30. Accessed September 28, 2019. Available at http://www.theguardian.com/world/2011/nov/30/occupy-wall-street-women-voices.

Melucci, Alberto. 1985. "The Symbolic Challenge of Social Movements." *Social Research* 52 (4): 789–816.

Messner, Michael A. 1997. *Politics of Masculinities: Men in Movements*. Thousand Oaks, CA: SAGE.

Meyer, David S., and Nancy Whittier. 1994. "Social Movement Spillover." *Social Problems* 41 (2): 277–298.

Milkman, Ruth. 2017. "A New Political Generation: Millennials and the Post-2008 Wave of Protest." *American Sociological Review* 82 (1): 1–31.

Milkman, Ruth, Stephanie Luce, and Penny Lewis. 2013. *Changing the Subject: A Bottom-Up Account of Occupy Wall Street in New York City*. New York: City University of New York Murphy Institute.

Mills, C. Wright. 1959. *The Sociological Imagination*. Oxford: Oxford University Press.

Montoya, Celeste. 2019. "From Identity Politics to Intersectionality? Identity-Based Organizing in the Occupy Movements." In *Gendered Mobilizations and Intersectional Challenges: Contemporary Social Movements in Europe and North America*, edited by Jill Irvine, Sabine Lang, and Celeste Montoya, 135–153. London: Rowman and Littlefield.

Moraga, Cherríe. 2011. *A Xicana Codex of Changing Consciousness: Writings, 2000–2010*. Durham, NC: Duke University Press.

Morin, Rich. 2012. "Rising Share of Americans See Conflict between Rich and Poor." *PEW Research Center*, January 11. Accessed April 11, 2019. Available at http://www.pewsocialtrends.org/2012/01/11/rising-share-of-americans-see-conflict-between-rich-and-poor/.

Morris, Aldon D. 1986. *The Origins of the Civil Rights Movement: Black Communities Organizing for Change*. New York: Free Press.

Morris, Aldon D., and Suzanne Staggenborg. 2004. "Leadership in Social Movements." In *The Blackwell Companion to Social Movements*, edited by David A. Snow, Sarah A. Soule, and Hanspeter Kriesi, 171–196. Oxford: Blackwell.

National Association of Real Estate Brokers (NAREB). 2013. "The State of Housing in Black America." *NAREB*, August 6. Accessed April 13, 2015. Available at http://issuu.com/jenningslj/docs/shiba_report_for_posting/1.

National Public Radio Staff and Wires. 2011. "Hundreds Arrested after Protest on Brooklyn Bridge." *National Public Radio*, October 1. Accessed November 18, 2014. Available at http://www.npr.org/2011/10/01/140983353/about-500-arrested-after-protest-on-brooklyn-bridge.

Newcomb, Alyssa. 2011. "Sexual Assaults Reported in 'Occupy' Camps." *ABC News/World News*, November 3. Accessed September 28, 2019. Available at http://abcnews.go.com/US/sexual-assaults-occupy-wall-street-camps/story?id=14873014.

Okechukwu, Amaka. 2014. "Shadows of Solidarity: Identity, Intersectionality, and Frame Resonance." In *Intersectionality and Social Change, Research in Social Movements, Conflicts and Change*, vol. 37, edited by Lynne M. Woehrle, 153–180. Bingly, UK: Emerald Group.

Oliver, Melvin. 2008. "Sub-prime as a Black Catastrophe." *American Prospect*, September 20. Accessed April 13, 2015. Available at https://prospect.org/article/sub-prime-black-catastrophe.

Oliver, Melvin L., and Thomas M. Shapiro. 2006. *Black Wealth, White Wealth: A New Perspective on Racial Inequality*. Abingdon, UK: Taylor and Francis.

Pedulla, David S., and Sarah Thébaud. 2015. "Can We Finish the Revolution? Gender, Work-Family Ideals, and Institutional Constraint." *American Sociological Review* 80 (1): 116–139.

Pick, Katharina. 2017. "Women, Leadership, and Power." In *Handbook of Research on Gender and Leadership*, edited by Susan Madsen, 223–237. Cheltenham, UK: Edward Elgar.

Pickard, Sarah, and Judith Bessant. 2018. "France's #Nuit Debout Social Movement: Young People Rising Up and Moral Emotions." *Societies* 8 (4): 1–21.

Pickerill, Jenny, and John Krinsky. 2012. "Why Does Occupy Matter?" *Social Movement Studies* 11 (3–4): 279–287.

Piven, Frances Fox. 2013. "On the Organizational Question." *Sociological Quarterly* 54 (2): 191–193.

———. 2014. "Interdependent Power: Strategizing for the Occupy Movement." *Current Sociology* 62 (2): 223–231.

Polletta, Francesca. 1999. "'Free Spaces' in Collective Action." *Theory and Society* 28 (1): 1–38.

———. 2002. *Freedom Is an Endless Meeting: Democracy in American Social Movements*. Chicago: University of Chicago.

Polletta, Francesca, and Katt Hoban. 2016. "Why Consensus? Prefiguration in Three Activist Eras." *Journal of Social and Political Psychology* 4 (1): 286–301.

Polletta, Francesca, and Kelsy Kretschmer. 2013. "Free Spaces." In *The Wiley-Blackwell Encyclopedia of Social and Political Movements*, edited by David A. Snow, Donatella della Porta, Bert Klandermans, and Doug McAdam, 1–5. Oxford: Wiley-Blackwell.

Porter, Tony. 2005. *Globalization and Finance*. New York: Polity Press.

Quinn, Sarah. 2011. "How a Few Bad Apples Turned into Several Bushels." *Occupied Stories*, November 9. Accessed February 6, 2012. Available at http://occupiedstories.com/how-a-few-bad-apples-turned-into-several-bushels.html.

Reger, Jo. 2012. *Everywhere and Nowhere: Contemporary Feminism in the United States*. New York: Oxford University Press.

———. 2015. "The Story of a Slut Walk: Sexuality, Race, and Generational Divisions in Contemporary Feminist Activism." *Journal of Contemporary Ethnography* 44 (1): 84–112.

Reich, Robert B. 2011. *Aftershock: The Next Economy and America's Future*. New York: Vintage.

Reissman, Catherine K. 1993. *Narrative Analysis*. London: SAGE.

Reuters. 2013. "Occupy Wall Street Lawsuits: NYC Agrees to Pay Protesters for Destroying Library, Property." *Huffington Post*, April 9. Accessed November 19, 2014. Available at http://www.huffingtonpost.com/2013/04/09/occupy-wall-street-lawsuits-nyc-library-property_n_3048772.html.

Ridgeway, Celia L. 2011. *Framed by Gender: How Gender Inequality Persists in the Modern World*. New York: Oxford University Press.

Rios, Victor. 2011. *Punished: Policing the Lives of Black and Latino Boys*. New York: New York University Press.

Robnett, Belinda. 1997. *How Long? How Long? African-American Women in the Struggle for Civil Rights*. New York: Oxford University Press.

Rohlinger, Deana A., and Elyse Claxton. 2017. "Mobilizing the Faithful: Conservative and Right-Wing Women's Movements in America." In *The Oxford Handbook of U.S. Women's Social Movement Activism*, edited by Holly J. McCammon, Lee Ann Banaszak, Verta Taylor, and Jo Reger, 150–171. New York: Oxford University Press.

Rose-Redwood, Cindy Ann, and Reuben Rose-Redwood. 2017. "'It Definitely Felt Very White': Race, Gender, and the Performative Politics of Assembly at the Women's March in Victoria, British Columbia." *Gender, Place and Culture* 24 (5): 645–654.

Rosette, Ashleigh Shelby, Christy Zhou Koval, Anyi Ma, and Robert Livingston. 2016. "Race Matters for Women Leaders: Intersectional Effects on Agentic Deficiencies and Penalties." *Leadership Quarterly* 27 (3): 429–445.

Roth, Benita. 2004. *Separate Roads to Feminism: Black, Chicana, and White Feminist Movements in America's Second Wave*. Cambridge: Cambridge University Press.

———. 2017. *The Life and Death of ACT UP/LA: Anti-AIDS Activism in Los Angeles from the 1980s to the 2000s*. Cambridge: Cambridge University Press.

Roth, Louise Marie. 2006. *Selling Women Short: Gender and Money on Wall Street*. Princeton, NJ: Princeton University Press.

Rüdig, Wolfgang, and Georgios Karyotis. 2013a. "Beyond the Usual Suspects? New Participants in Anti-austerity Protests in Greece." *Mobilization: An International Quarterly* 18 (3): 313–330.

———. 2013b. "Who Protests in Greece? Mass Opposition to Austerity." *British Journal of Political Science* 44 (3): 487–513.

Rudman, Laurie A., and Kimberly Fairchild. 2004. "Reactions to Counterstereotypic Behavior: The Role of Backlash in Cultural Stereotype Maintenance." *Journal of Personality and Social Psychology* 87 (2): 157–176.

Rudman, Laurie A., and Kris Mescher. 2013. "Penalizing Men Who Request a Family Leave: Is Flexibility Stigma a Femininity Stigma?" *Journal of Social Issues* 69 (2): 322–340.

Rupp, Leila J., and Verta Taylor. 1999. "Forging Feminist Identity in an International Movement: A Collective Identity Approach to Feminism." *Signs: Journal of Women in Culture and Society* 24 (2): 363–386.

———. 2003. *Drag Queens at the 801 Cabaret*. Chicago: University of Chicago Press.

———. 2011. "Going Back and Giving Back: The Ethics of Staying in the Field." *Qualitative Sociology: Special Issue: Ethics: Beyond the IRB* 34 (3): 483–496.

Salime, Zakia. 2012. "A New Feminism? Gender Dynamics in Morocco's February 20th Movement." *Journal of International Women's Studies* 13 (5): 101–114.

Sandberg, Sheryl, and Adam Grant. 2015. "Speaking While Female." *New York Times*, January 12. Accessed February 27, 2018. Available at http://nyti.ms/1A7Xwyw.

Schein, Rebecca. 2012. "Whose Occupation? Homelessness and the Politics of Park Encampments." *Social Movement Studies* 11 (3–4): 335–341.

Schippers, Mimi. 2002. *Rockin' out of the Box: Gender Maneuvering in Alternative Hard Rock*. New Brunswick, NJ: Rutgers University Press.

Schneider, Nathan. 2013. *Thank You, Anarchy: Notes from the Occupy Apocalypse*. Berkeley: University of California Press.

Seltzer, Sarah. 2011. "Where Are the Women at Occupy Wall Street? They're Everywhere." In *The 99%: How the Occupy Wall Street Movement Is Changing America*, edited by Lynn Parramore, Tara Lohan, and Don Hazen, 80–84. San Francisco: AlterNet.

Shaw, Sylvia. 2000. "Language, Gender and Floor Apportionment in Political Debates." *Discourse and Society* 11 (3): 401–418.

Sitrin, Marina A. 2012a. *Everyday Revolutions: Horizontalism and Autonomy in Argentina*. London: Zed Books Ltd.

———. 2012b. "Horizontalism and the Occupy Movements." *Dissent* 59 (2): 74–75.

Smith, Dorothy E. 2005. *Institutional Ethnography: A Sociology for People*. Lanham, MD: Altamira.

Smith, Ellie. 2011. "Women's Caucus." *Occupy! An OWS-Inspired Gazette* 1: 9–10.

Smith, Jackie, and Bob Glidden. 2012. "Occupy Pittsburgh and the Challenges of Participatory Democracy." *Social Movement Studies* 11 (3–4): 288–294.

Snow, David. 2004. "Framing Processes, Ideology, and Discursive Fields." In *The Blackwell Companion to Social Movements*, edited by David A. Snow, Sarah A. Soule, and Hanspeter Kriesi, 380–412. Oxford: Blackwell.

Sprague, Joey. 2005. *Feminist Methodologies for Critical Researchers: Bridging Differences*. Lanham, MD: Altamira.

Staggenborg, Suzanne, and Verta Taylor. 2005. "Whatever Happened to the Women's Movement?" *Mobilization: An International Quarterly* 10 (1): 37–52.

Stevens, Angi Becker. 2011. "We Are the 99%, Too: Creating a Feminist Space within Occupy Wall Street." *Ms.*, October 11. Accessed September 28, 2019. Available at https://msmagazine.com/2011/10/11/we-are-the-99-too-creating-a-feminist-space-within-occupy-wall-street/.

Sturm, Susan. 2001. "Second-Generation Employment Discrimination: A Structural Approach." *Columbia Law Review* 101 (3): 458–568.

Swidler, Ann. 1986. "Culture in Action: Symbols and strategies." *American Sociological Review* 51 (2): 273–286.

Taibbi, Matt. 2011. *Griftopia: A Story of Bankers, Politicians, and the Most Audacious Power Grab in American History*. New York: Spiegel and Grau.

Tannen, Deborah. 1995. "The Power of Talk: Who Gets Heard and Why." *Harvard Business Review* 73 (5): 138–148.

Taylor, Verta. 1989. "Social Movement Continuity: The Women's Movement in Abeyance." *American Sociological Review* 54 (5): 761–775.

———. 1996. *Rock-a-By Baby: Feminism, Self-Help, and Postpartum Depression*. New York: Routledge.

———. 1998. "Feminist Methodology in Social Movements Research." *Qualitative Sociology* 21 (4): 357–379.

———. 1999. "Gender and Social Movements: Gender Processes in Women's Self-Help Movements." *Gender & Society* 13 (1): 8–33.

Taylor, Verta, and Leila J. Rupp. 1993. "Women's Culture and Lesbian Feminist Activism: A Reconsideration of Cultural Feminism." *Signs: Journal of Women in Culture and Society* 19 (1): 32–61.

———. 2005. "Crossing Boundaries in Participatory Action Research: Performing Protest with Drag Queens." In *Rhyming Hope and History: Activism and Social Movement Scholarship*, edited by David Croteau, William Hoynes, and Charlotte Ryan, 239–264. Minneapolis: University of Minnesota Press.

Taylor, Verta, and Nancy Whittier. 1992. "Collective Identity in Social Movement Communities: Lesbian Feminist Mobilization." In *Frontiers in Social Movement Theory*, edited by Aldon Morris and Carol Mueller, 104–129. New Haven, CT: Yale University Press.

———. 1995. "Analytical Approaches to Social Movement Culture: The Culture of the Women's Movement." In *Social Movements and Culture*, edited by Hank Johnston and Bert Klandermans, 163–187. Minneapolis: University of Minnesota Press.

Tepper, Bennett J., Michelle Duffy, and Jason Shaw. 2001. "Personality Moderators of the Relationship between Abusive Supervision and Subordinates' Resistance." *Journal of Applied Psychology* 86 (5): 974–983.

Terriquez, Veronica. 2015. "Intersectional Mobilization, Social Movement Spillover, and Queer Youth Leadership in the Immigrant Rights Movement." *Social Problems* 62 (3): 343–362.

Tormos, F. 2017. "Intersectional Solidarity." *Politics, Groups, and Identities* 5 (4): 707–720.

Townsend-Bell, Erica. 2011. "What Is Relevance? Defining Intersectional Praxis in Uruguay." *Political Research Quarterly* 64 (1): 187–199.

Upton, Aisha A., and Joyce M. Bell. 2017. "Women's Activism in the Modern Movement for Black Liberation." In *The Oxford Handbook of U.S. Women's Social Movement Activism*, edited by Holly J. McCammon, Lee Ann Banaszak, Verta Taylor, and Jo Reger, 623–642. New York: Oxford University Press.

Van Stekelenburg, Jacquelien. 2012. "The Occupy Movement: Product of This Time." *Development* 55 (2): 224–231.

Vial, Andrea, Jaime Napier, and Victoria Brescoll. 2016. "A Bed of Thorns: Female Leaders and the Self-Reinforcing Cycle of Illegitimacy." *Leadership Quarterly* 27 (3): 400–414.

Welsh, Sandy. 1999. "Gender and Sexual Harassment." *Annual Review of Sociology* 25 (1): 169–190.

West, Candace, and Don H. Zimmerman. 1987. "Doing Gender." *Gender & Society* 1 (2): 125–151.

Wettergren, Asa. 2005. "Mobilization and the Moral Shock: Adbusters Media Foundation." In *Emotions and Social Movements*, edited by Helena Flam and Deborah King, 99–118. New York: Routledge.

Whittier, Nancy. 2012. "The Politics of Coming Out: Visibility and Identity in Activism against Child Sexual Abuse." In *Strategies for Social Change*, edited by Gregory M. Maney, Rachel V. Kutz-Flamenbaum, Deanna A. Rohlinger, and Jeff Goodwin, 145–169. Minneapolis: University of Minnesota Press.

Wilkinson, Richard, and Kate Pickett. 2009. *The Spirit Level: Why Greater Equality Makes Societies Stronger*. New York: Bloomsbury Press.

Wollan, Malia. 2011. "Oakland's Port Shuts Down as Protesters March on Waterfront." *New York Times*, November 2. Accessed November 19, 2014. Available at http://www.nytimes.com/2011/11/03/us/occupy-oakland-protesters-set-sights-on-closing-port.html.

Young, Iris Marion. 1997. *Intersecting Voices: Dilemmas of Gender, Political Philosophy, and Policy*. Princeton, NJ: Princeton University Press.

Index

Journal, 72, 140; *Occupy! N+1,* 76, 77, 108, 116, 156; photography, 33, 67; same-sex marriage and, 53; #SayHer-Name, 11; social media, 5, 16, 22, 32, 38–39, 55, 62, 64, 140–142, 144; white male dominance and, 15, 46, 93–94, 105, 147, 149; Women's Media Center, 116; working groups, 52, 104–105; zines, 55, 62, 95, 101, 107. *See also* Framing; Inclusivity frames; InterOc-cupy; Online activism

Meetings, 3, 7, 18–20, 22–23, 26, 58, 74, 102, 151–152; feminist, 68, 113, 125, 130; inclusive, 36, 46, 55, 83; leadership and, 91–92; progressive stack and, 105; sexism and racism and, 52, 95–100, 116, 128–129, 132; social media and, 64. *See also* General assemblies; Working groups

Membership, 12–13, 129, 146, 149. *See also* Recruitment

Men, cisgender and transgender. *See* Gender; LGBTQ

Messerschmidt, James, 78

Mic check, 2, 41–42, 102–103, 138; tran-scription process, 155, 157

Milkman, Ruth, 16, 20, 133, 155

Millennials, 2, 17, 40, 114, 125, 138–139; Millennials for Bernie, 140–141; orga-nizing online, 16, 62, 133

Mixed-race participants, 40, 46, 100, 104, 153, 164n3–4

Monist analyses, 10, 12, 14, 34–39, 63, 69, 146

Morgan, Robin, 116

Murphy, Susan, 106

Music, 1, 23, 66, 72, 106–107, 115; drum-ming, 41; Guitarmy, 59–60, 106–107; Mr. Holland's Opus Foundation, 60; Rage Against the Machine, 106; sing-ing, 26, 37, 55, 72, 102–103

Napier, Jaime, 108

NatGat (Occupy National Gathering), 20–22, 25–26, 103, 153, 158–159; 99 Mile March and, 59–60; feminism and, 84, 96–97, 120–121, 127; LGBTQ and, 54

Networks, 3, 6, 16, 31–34, 67, 136, 141; black churches, 42; feminist, 28, 67, 114–116, 127, 129–130; InterOc-cupy, 81; LGBTQ, 130; networking opportunities, 94; online, 16, 18, 30, 133, 140. *See also* Media; Online activism

New Left movement, 93, 100, 113

New York City, New York, 1–2, 6, 17–18, 21–23, 37–38, 133–134; *The Declara-tion of the Occupation of New York City,* 72–73, 77; feminist, 113–114, 117–119, 122–123, 125–126; LGBTQ, 54; "the Muslim ban" protest, 148; participants, 36, 46, 50–51, 59–60, 84, 97, 104; September 17, 2012 protest, 73–74, 115; Stock Exchange, 22, 140; Zuccotti Park, 1, 18, 22–23, 38, 52, 61, 72, 125, 140. *See also* 99 Mile March; Alternative Banking Working Group; *Charging Bull;* CODEPINK; Guitarmy; Harassment; Homeless persons and groups; Occupy Sandy; Occupy Wall Street; Raging Grannies; Safer Spaces; Sanders, Bernie; Stop and frisk; Tax Dodgers and the Corporate Loop-holes; Wall Street; Women Occupying Wall Street (WOWS)

New York General Assembly. *See* Occupy Wall Street

Nuit Debout, 144

Oakland, California 21, 23–25, 66; anarchists, 76; Asian Immigrant Women Advocates (AIWA), 11–12; Commune, 24–27; harassment, 99; Occupy Patriarchy, 118–119, 125–126, participants, 37, 95, 100–101; port, 38, 119; strike, 119. *See also* Decolonize; Indigenous persons; Oakland Occupy Patriarchy; Occupy the Farm; Occupy Oakland

Oakland Occupy Patriarchy, 118–119, 125–126

Obama, Barack, 77

Occupy Central with Peace and Love, 144

Occupy National Gathering. *See* NatGat

Heather McKee Hurwitz is a Lecturer of Sociology and feminist scholar at Case Western Reserve University and a Visiting Researcher at the Cleveland Clinic.